MANAGEMENT AUDITS FOR EXCELLENCE

MANAGEMENT AUDITS FOR EXCELLENCE

**The Manager's Guide to Improving the Quality
and Productivity of an Organization**

Dorsey J. Talley

ASQC Quality Press
American Society for Quality Control
310 West Wisconsin Avenue
Milwaukee, Wisconsin 53203

Published by ASQC Quality Press

MANAGEMENT AUDITS FOR EXCELLENCE

The Manager's Guide to Improving the Quality
and Productivity of an Organization

Dorsey J. Talley

Copyright © 1988
by ASQC Quality Press

ISBN 0-87389-039-6

ACKNOWLEDGMENTS

Without the total support of my family, Bessie Hodge Talley Warren, Rhonda Lynne Talley, James Eric (Jet) Talley, and especially my wife Norma Arnold Talley, none of the many projects would have been completed.

The outstanding education, training, and experiences that the U.S. Air Force has provided for me during 26 years of active duty helped make this book possible.

Thanks to all the team players who, over the years, helped me to get "A" scores/completions on the jobs, tasks, audits, and reviews, and to attain the rank of colonel in the USAF. Specifically, LTC Jim Spearman, Col. Willie Sonntag, Col. Frank Bossembark, Capt. (USN) Walt Tolson, Col. John Mehwa, Maj. Gen. "Tex" Reilly, Maj. Gen. Mert Baker, and the many others.

Thanks to General Dynamics' faith and trust in recognizing my abilities and talents in the management triad of technical, interpersonal, and administrative skills.

Special caveats for the ideas, help, reviews, and editing of this book go to Don Patterson, Jim Coburn, Jim Mayben, Fred Guardia, Maj. Gen. Mert Baker, my administrative assistant, Mary Harper, and my executive secretary, Janet Hoggatt, the ultimate in a person and fellow worker, without whose outstanding efforts you would not be reading this book.

Thanks to you all! Talley-Ho!

TABLE OF CONTENTS

PREFACE

The Arena

"It is not the critic who counts, nor the man who points out how the strong man stumbled, or where the doer of deeds could have done them better. The credit belongs to the man who is actually in the arena; whose face is marred by dust and sweat and blood who strives valiantly; who errs and comes short again and again, who knows the great enthusiasms, the great devotions; who spreads himself in a worthy cause; who, at the best, knows in the end the triumph of high achievement; and who, at the worst, if he fails, at least fails while daring greatly."

President Theodore Roosevelt

ONE

Introduction

Every conscientious manager, director, vice president, or general manager eventually stops on the golf course, or relaxes under a pine tree during an infrequent vacation, and asks the inevitable questions: Why didn't I know what my managers were doing in the engineering, production, quality, etc., departments? How did they manage their particular functions, what were their key indicators, and how did they measure productivity gains? Did they have people programs to motivate personnel? Were they really aware of the total performance of their groups' activities? These questions, and others the readers should add, need to be asked, answered, and evaluated to achieve top performance.

This book offers a slightly different concept to give top management of a company or department a way to personally audit each functional organization and determine how well it can be expected to perform. In the United States and most of the business world countries, top management does not use nor have an adequate method of evaluating the true health of their organizations. In the January 1987 issue of *Quality Progress*, Komatsu chairman Ryorihi Kawai explains the reason for personally auditing his plants: ". . . the plant managers reported what I wanted to hear." Komatsu conducts a top management quality control audit every year as part of total quality control activities. Oliver C. Boileau, president of General Dynamics Corporation, became convinced in 1981 that the reports and quarterly reviews were not enough to truly feel the pulse of the 20 operating divisions. Too many problems kept surfacing that could have been prevented. He started annual corporate top management reviews and basically uses the techniques that are developed in this book with expanded checklists. This tool is called the management assessment program (MAP). It provides a systematic auditing and evaluating process that gives management a total performance picture. Few companies have a management information system (MIS) illuminating enough to measure total monthly or quarterly performance.

In my many years of working for the Department of Defense, the U.S. Air Force, and a large multidivision aerospace manufacturing company, I have been privileged to conduct many studies, management audits, specific functional audits, and problem analyses dealing with the hows and whys of management. During the past 12 years, I have learned the hard way that there are very few books, manuals, or guides on how to conduct a top management audit. For each particular review or audit I needed to design, develop, and tailor a new set of guidelines and checklists.

This book is basically a how-to-do-it manual. The ideas are practical, not theoretical. They form an action plan aimed at assisting you to achieve excellence — "qualitivity," productivity, and profitability. In doing that, you will be helping this great country stay great and meet the competitive forces that challenge us from all directions. The key performance in this action is you. Rather than watch what happens, you must influence what happens. Check it out yourself — isn't that what management and leadership are all about?

Management Responsibilities

Why Excellence?

Plenty has gone wrong in American industry, and top management is too far removed from the details to do more than detect the fact that there are problems. Unfortunately, mergers and oversized organizations have unleashed a negative synergy, and top management finds itself pulled even further away from the product and the customer. Now, industry finds it has to do a better job of managing the entire innovation process. It needs to make smart investments in the development of new products and new equipment. It needs to produce better results from existing facilities. It needs more top involvement in manufacturing decisions, more emphasis on technology planning in corporate strategy, and more people development — because quality depends on trained and motivated people.

Unfortunately, things are out of synch. There is a mismatch between the needs and the attitudes and interests of our current managerial talent. Far too many managers see their companies as potential money machines rather than engines for generating quality products.[1] People drawn to the top of a company have relied primarily on the "hard" tools of return on investment, earnings per share, cost per unit, etc. People, values, ethics, and quality have become the "soft" background subjects which are either of little importance or elude management control.

However, in the 1980s, CEOs have begun to realize that the keys to a company's success, large or small, lie in a commitment to (1) business ethics, (2) people, (3) quality, and (4) customer service. It is time for American executives to establish a firm ethical foundation in companies that can help executives and managers deal with issues that otherwise would not be clear issues.[2] Currently, the headlines are full of unethical business news — excessive profits, gross spares and warranties pricing applications, accounting irregularities to raise or lower earnings, and kickbacks on sales. Integrity is a must for American managers, who are frustrated by grappling with the myriad of problems their industries face.

Some observers of American management have long suspected that the key to the survival and prosperity of their companies — large and small — lies not in the rational, quantitative approach to problem solving so popular in the 1960s and 1970s, but rather in a commitment to irrational, difficult-to-measure things like quality, people, and customer service. Peters and Waterman stated in their book, *In Search of Excellence*, that 62 of the "best run" companies have found these elusive differences. They emphasize ethics, integrity, superior quality, and service, and they value people as individuals. These companies consistently exhibit the following attributes of excellence:

- A bias for action.
- Closeness to the customer.

- Autonomy and entrepreneurship.
- Belief in productivity through people.
- A hands-on, value-driven operation.
- A tendency to "stick to the knitting."
- A simple form and lean staff.
- Simultaneous, loose-tight properties — autonomy at the shop-floor level combined with fanatic adherence to certain ideas.[3]

Leadership

Where is the leadership in the public or private sector that will point the country in the right direction and that has the vision to see down the road 20 years? We had that kind of vision when we as a nation made the decision to go to the moon. Where is the leadership in the private sector that says quality and productivity are the long-range goals of the company? Many companies are reacting to the crisis they are in, but few can say they have had a long commitment to total quality. The business community as a whole isn't providing the nation with the leadership that it needs in this area. Where is the leadership that will give us the direction and vision to redirect the country's lagging educational system? Where is the leadership among professional groups that will force them to consider the greater good of the country instead of their own narrow interests? I don't see any of that leadership that can help us address our problems in a proactive manner; hence, I feel it will take a disaster of sorts to focus the attention of the nation on the problems of quality and productivity. Improving quality and productivity can no longer be mundane to anyone in any business organization or country.

"The average American is unaware of the real seriousness of our nation's and businesses' struggle for survival and the real challenge to his present way of life. He does not understand or realize how much of our productivity or value added is actually accomplished in foreign countries; nor is he aware of how many U.S. companies and associated resources are actually foreign owned. He is inappreciative of the fact that business should reward high performance and punish low performance of its employees. He sees low performance rewarded to the same extent in many instances as high performance and starts wondering why he is trying so hard to do an outstanding job. His government sets barriers in trade to protect his livelihood when the real answer lies in competition. He sees himself surrounded in waste — doing things a second time because they were not accomplished with excellence the first time; having to put up with products and services which are not what they should be and he places his own resources in the breach to make them better. He should demand better as an American at his place of employment, in the marketplace, in his children's schools, in our judicial system, etc."[4]

Management Policy

Companies and large divisions of corporations have their own distinctive operating style, but for any type of management to succeed, certain characteristics must be present. Management's policy must be clear and understood by both the formal and informal organization. (Formal organization is that which is laid out by the procedures and organizational charts. Informal organization is that which is actually practiced due to the perceived power of the key players of mid-management.) A statement of the company's objectives gives people a sense of values by which to work and live. It suggests ways to behave in the organization and ways for the organization to behave in response to its people, its customers, and the communities it serves.[5] Management objectives should address the following:

- People — Each person receives recognition he or she needs and deserves.
- Customers — The highest levels of honesty, integrity, and responsiveness are maintained in meeting merchandise and service needs.
- Quality — Quality products and services commensurate with the standards demanded by our customers are provided.
- Fields of Endeavor — New fields are entered only when the ideas, and technical, manufacturing, and marketing skills ensure that a needed and profitable contribution can be made to the field.
- Management — Initiative and creativity is fostered by allowing individuals great freedom of action in attaining well-defined objectives.
- Citizenship and Business Conduct — A consistently high standard of business conduct, ethics, and social responsibility is maintained to honor obligations to the nation and the community.
- Growth — Growth is limited only by profits and ability to develop and produce products that satisfy real customer needs.
- Profit — Each product is designed and developed so that it is considered a good value by customers, yet is priced to include an adequate profit.

Quality Awareness Survey

There are many ways to improve quality and productivity, and many management techniques that work in different situations. There are many indicators and MISs for measuring performance and the financial health of an organization. But what is the best way to get it all together and find out how your organization actually is running?

Ask the people! An employee opinion survey can directly assist you in determining the validity of the systems and supervision expertise that have you at your current level of performance. Appendix A shows a quality improvement program survey that was developed and conducted at General Dynamics to correct and eliminate any significant obstacles to optimum quality and productivity.

Try something like the quality improvement program survey approach in your company, division, or department. You might just be surprised enough to do things differently.

Stay on Top with Audits
Task Audits

In today's complex business environment, all executives delegate to some degree. Styles of delegation range all the way from the executive who turns over an assignment carte blanche to the executive who treats subordinates as assistants, giving them a minimum of authority and responsibility. But, no matter how much authority and responsibility is delegated, the executive, not the subordinate, possesses full accountability for the task, job, department, profit, etc. So how can an executive keep up with what is happening in the company, division, department, and lower levels of supervision?

In the *Harvard Business Review*, James Harrison cites several methods of auditing job assignments[7]:

- Previewing Directives — The executive and subordinate work to a plan of action that includes milestones.
- Questioning on Progress — The executive sends for or goes to subordinates at varying times; requires deft timing and a clear attitude of friendly interest by the executive.
- Demanding Reports — The subordinate submits periodic progress reports, with or without specific deadlines. This method relies heavily on the subordinate's talents and the executive's clarity in putting across the original ideas.
- Scheduling Conferences — This is most useful when the project is one that has a series of events that can be planned and tried in advance; combines questioning on progress and demanding reports.
- Setting Deadlines — The executive uses this only when subordinates have proven their ability to perform successfully, their modes of performance are identical to that of the delegating executive, or the task is so perfunctory that the path to its completion is unmistakable.
- Checking Results — This method, unlike questioning on progress, can be used only when the project has tangible results while in progress. This is the most accurate, most convenient for all, and the least trouble to the subordinate.
- Measuring by Crosscurrents — Crosscurrents of work flow provide measuring devices and warning signals if an executive is attuned to them.

Management Audits

The larger picture of auditing the results of total organizational performance stresses the true executive's capabilities. Most organizations have the means to conduct financial audits by a corporate internal audit group, operations audits by the quality assurance audit group, and performance audits by the industrial relations group. But very few organizations actually do a management audit. Occasionally, a corporate problem audit team descends when there is a large problem defined by the customer, but executives and managers need to know how well they and their organization are doing on an everyday basis.

The management audit is *forward-looking*, to see how well management is accomplishing its objectives and to spot operational difficulties before the fact, rather than after the fact as with a financial audit. This forward-looking approach is analogous to the preventive maintenance concept found in production. Periodic management audits can pinpoint problems as they are developing from a small scale.[8] A second important benefit is that it represents another, and perhaps the most important, *management tool* to assist the organization in accomplishing desired objectives. It can pinpoint those major bottlenecks prior to disaster. If certain managers are ineffective in their present positions, appropriate corrective action should be taken. A third benefit of the management audit technique is that it is an *objective appraisal* based on factual evidence that can be tracked for problem resolution.

Participation — The Key to Success

Any successful audit (*management review* may be a better term to still the auditee's fearful heart) requires teamwork and cooperation. The MAP checklists discussed in this book should be given to the auditee. The auditee then can do a self-appraisal, answer the questions in writing, and have the necessary documentation at hand — records, procedures, forms, and reports. This allows those most knowledgeable of each operating function and division to accomplish the preliminary groundwork. It serves a subtler purpose as well. If the operating manager responsible for answering the review questions knows the answers, then the shop should be in good shape. But if the manager cannot respond, then he or she needs to take a good hard look at operations before pursuing acceptable standards.

The BOSS Connection

The BOSS (big one on site surveillance) connection is a significant psychological aspect of running the business. Leadership, audits, and participation we have already discussed, but it needs to be emphasized over and over, people want to see, feel, and hear the boss! So to be effective in getting the quality and productivity out of your organization — BOSS it!

Reports from a well-defined MIS are necessary, but we have to be tuned into performance, and we must demand performance. How do we do this? One technique that has been copied from many other successful managers is the BOSS technique — meandering around the production floor, the engineering laboratories, the flight line, and the material department, observing, talking to the company personnel, asking questions about the inputs to the reports received, and asking questions about their productivity and quality output. Don't let yourself be so tied down by the paperwork, the meetings, and the telephone that you don't have time to BOSS it. Take an hour each day to visit some department, work center, or area — don't schedule these, just get up and go out on the floor.

Reports, committees, operating procedures, and objectives are all necessary, but they should be used correctly to make the organization run smoothly. Make sure that you read the reports — make comments and send them back, question actions of the committees, and track the objectives. If you do not use some type of MAP audits and BOSS techniques, you will not be challenging your people.

TWO

The Audit Technique

Management Assessment Program

The MAP concept, some precepts, and management questions are partially derived from the U.S. Air Force Contractor Management System Evaluation Program.[10] The idea behind MAP is to provide a reliable, effective, systematic management technique to detect existing and potential problems, and generate a timely corrective action system. MAP is based on the fundamental principle that *product quality is the direct result of management quality* starting at the top of a company's organization. It is also based on the assumption that a responsible company, dedicated to the delivery of a quality product within cost and on schedule, will develop and document a MIS in an orderly and planned manner, ensure that all functional organizations understand the system, and validate compliance with it through an effective internal self-audit. The MAP audit technique is question-based to determine if a system or condition exists, if it is adequate, and if the organization/persons are complying with the situation/standard. Figure 1 illustrates the basic flow of the MAP process.

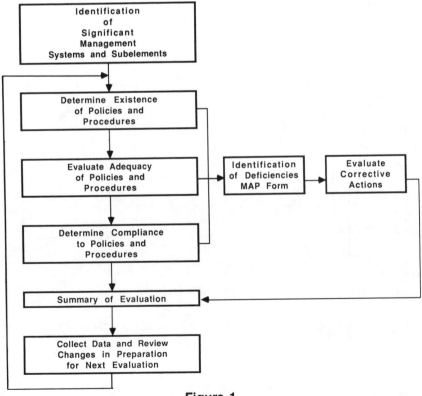

Figure 1
General Overview of MAP

9

A format has been developed that will guide the reviewer through the functional areas (Figure 2). The checklist areas will be discussed in detail, starting with the general manager to the service organization in the field. Much of the organizational entities discussed in this book will center around a defense-oriented company, but the technique is universally applicable to any company, division, or department.

Management Assessment Program

Page of Pages

Area	Organization	Supervisor	Dates	
			Now	
			Next Audit	

Functional Area Question	Existence		Adequate		Compliance		Correction Required			Closed Sat. Date
	Y	N	Y	N	Y	N	By	Task Team Required	Response Due Date	

Figure 2
MAP Format

To ensure effective use of the MAP concept, it is best to establish a plan of audits with early emphasis on those areas that appear to be in trouble. It is best to complete the first pass through the major parts of the organization for an effective baseline — then you know where you are. But you will not continue the knowledge of effective progress unless you have used this checklist and others to develop an effective MIS.

Key Management Information System Indicators

An in-depth MIS and a hands-on approach to working with your people are the keys to excellence. Data are needed to predict the future for managers, not just report the past. It should be as simple as possible to collect and report, and the MIS should be kept short, so managers can spend more time with the people working on problems and less time on paperwork.

All department managers should have six to nine management by objectives (MBO) indicators for their department. These MBOs should be developed carefully, based on sound history, and have improvement targets in the 10 to 30 percent annual improvement ranges. Each executive vice-president should end up with 20 to 30 indicators; if there are more than 30, the indicators start losing their value.

What should you look at as the general manager of a manufacturing division? The following is an executive MIS listing for a large division with $500 million in annual sales.

Executive Management Information System

Primary	Secondary
I. Introduction and Matrix	
1. Major project status (e.g. MRP II, production facilitization and move, etc.)	
2. Watchlists	
a. supplier problems	
b. major hardware problems	
c. administrative hotspots	
d. customer concerns	
	e. etc.
II. Financial Status	
1. Division sales and earnings	
a. monthly cash flow	
	b. before tax profit
	c. gross sales
	d. cost of sales
	e. funded vs. unfunded backlog
f. withholdings (current/potential)	
2. Cost trends	
a. total division indirect cost	
	(1) indirect labor (including ratios)
	(2) indirect other
	(3) overtime
b. total division direct cost	
	(1) direct labor
	(2) direct material
	(3) direct other
	(4) overtime
	c. total division capital appropriations and expenditures
	(1) committed
	(2) spent
	(3) actual savings
	(4) allocation by department
	(5) contingency
d. allowable vs. unallowable cost posture	
	e. contract labor (manpower/cost)
	f. cost reduction programs
	(1) value engineering changes
	(2) employee suggestions
	(3) item documentations
3. Customer evaluations	
a. deficiency reports	
	b. department allocation and narrative
	c. most recent management review
4. Departmental (finance) status	
	a. manpower (direct/indirect/ % of division)
	b. total cost (direct/indirect)
c. overtime	

Executive Management Information System (cont.)

Primary	Secondary
III. Industrial Relations and Legal	

	1. Personnel trends
	   a. divisional direct/indirect manpower
	     levels

2. EEO, EPA, safety, etc.
   a. safety statistics
   b. hazardous waste	

	3. Employee trends
	   a. attrition
	   b. hires
	   c. college recruits

4. Security clearance a. violations	
	b. classification distribution

	5. Training
	   a. mandatory training
	     (actual vs. forecast)
	   b. budget vs. actual $
	   c. hours/exempt employee

6. Union relations
   a. grievances
     (1) open backlog	

	(2) average closure time
	     (3) number received vs. number
	        closed

7. Legal
   a. lawsuits
     (1) internal
     (2) external	

	(3) $ filed vs. $ settled (4) open vs. closed (backlog)

	8. Departmental (IR) status
	   a. manpower (direct/indirect/
	     % of division)
	   b. total cost (direct/indirect)

c. overtime	
IV. Marketing	
	1. Operating/strategic plan (performance to forecast)

2. Division master schedule roll-up
   (total business base)
   a. X business base summary
     (one page)
   b. Y business base summary
     (one page)	

	3. X business base detail
	   a. firm
	     (1) total cost/schedule
	   b. high potential
	     (1) total schedule
	4. Y detail
	   a. total cost/schedule
	     (firm/high potential)
	5. Z products detail
	   a. total cost/schedule
	     (firm/high potential)
	6. Other business

Executive Management Information System (cont.)

Primary	Secondary
V. X Program Status	
	1. Worldwide schedule
	2. Deliveries
	a. customer
	b. customer
	c. customer
	3. Performance to total cost target
4. Waivers and deviations	
5. Class I engineering change proposals	
6. Field performance	
a. mission capable rate	
	b. operational reliability
	c. operational maintainability
	d. abort rates
	e. sortie rates
	f. incident rates
	g. field retrofits
	7. Coproduction material dollar status
	8. Departmental status
	a. manpower (direct/indirect/ % of division)
	b. total cost (direct/indirect)
c. overtime	
VI. Y Program Status	
	1. Schedule performance (actual articles delivered vs. contract schedule)
	2. Cost performance
	3. Active programs
	a. restoration
	b. component repair
	c. I
	d. II
	e. XX
4. Engineering change proposals	
a. kit schedule	
b. retrofit schedule	
	5. Departmental status
	a. manpower (direct/indirect/ % of division)
	b. total cost (direct/indirect)
c. overtime	
VII. Electronic Products	
	1. Major contracts
	a. dollar value
	b. deliverables
	c. schedules
d. highlights	
	2. Departmental (electronic products) status
	a. manpower (direct/indirect/ % of division)
	b. total cost (direct/indirect)
c. overtime	

Executive Management Information System (cont.)

Primary	Secondary
VIII. Division Productivity	
1. Corporate quality improvement process parameters	

	2. All other quality improvement process
	       charts with trend analysis
	    3. Office automation status
	       a. schedule
	       b. costs
	       c. projects

IX. Quality
    1. Total nonconformance
       cost chart	

	2. Remainder of monthly GM pitch
	    3. Departmental (QA) status
	       a. manpower (direct/indirect/
	         % of division)
	       b. total cost (direct/indirect)

c. overtime	
X. Production	

	1. Schedule
	    2. Performance
	       a. hours/unit (learning curve)
	       b. man hours/pound

c. out-of-station hours
    d. work measurement performance
       to standard	

	3. Departmental production status
	       a. manpower (direct/indirect/
	         % of division)
	       b. total cost (direct/indirect)

c. overtime	

	d. other overhead accounts
	    4. Manufacturing control
	       a. shortages
	       b. critical ratio
	       c. orders in backlog
	       d. orders completed
	    5. Tool design backlog
	       (workable vs. nonworkable)

6. Tool manufacturing backlog	
XI. Research and Engineering 1. Major projects/priorities	
	2. Drawing release schedule 3. Hours/drawing

4. Class II engineering change notices
    5. Engineering liaison activity
    6. B&P/IRAD	

	7. Department (research and engineering)
	       status
	       a. manpower (direct/indirect/
	         % of division)
	       b. Total cost (direct/indirect)

c. overtime	

Executive Management Information System (cont.)

Primary	Secondary
XII. Logistics and Support	
1. Program X	
a. spares delivery	
b. kits delivery	
	c. support equipment and trainers delivery
	d. tech orders/data
e. service reports	
	f. sortie rates
	g. base structure
	h. customer training
	i. deployment (actual and projected)
	2. Program Y
	a. same as X above
	3. GFP schedule performance
	a. delivery to schedule
	b. other factors
4. Warranty information	
	5. Department (Logistics) status
	a. manpower (direct/indirect/ % of division)
	b. total cost (direct/indirect)
c. overtime	
XIII. Data Systems	
	1. Cost
	a. dollars
	b. direct and indirect hours
	c. capital
	(1) YTD actuals vs. forecast
	d. CAD-CAM statistics
e. productivity	
(1) man hours/CPU	
(2) $/CPU	
	f. CRAY/computer
g. hours/week/terminal (actual vs. objective)	
	2. Departmental (DSD/CC) status
	a. manpower (direct/indirect/ % of division)
	b. total cost (direct/indirect)
c. overtime	
XIV. Material	
	1. Cost
	a. performance to budget
	b. performance to budget (other)
	2. Schedule performance
	a. by contract (production only)
b. shortages	
3. Competition	
a. percent and dollar amount completed	
	b. sole source
	c. small business goals
	d. minority business goals

Executive Management Information System (cont.)

Primary	Secondary
4. Inventory a. actual vs. forecast	

	5. Department (material) status
	  a. manpower (direct/indirect/
	    % of division)
	  b. total cost (direct/indirect)

c. overtime	

XV. Contracts and Estimating
  1. X proposal status
    a. change
    b. production	

	2. Other proposal status 3. Dollar value undefinitized 4. Defective pricing claims

5. Withholding
    a. status and trends
      (1) claims
      (2) dollar value	

	6. Department (contracts and estimating)
	  a. manpower (direct/indirect/
	    % of division)
	  b. total cost (direct/indirect)

c. overtime	

General Management

Strategic Plan

Does the company have a plan that defines where the company wants to be in five to 20 years? The plan should address the product lines, the customer, and the market areas to be sought. It should also address the key strategies to reach the long-term objectives. Is the plan developed as a consensus of the total staff, or is it developed only by the marketing department and the general manager? Even though most companies have a strategic plan, it is often developed without the interplay with the material/procurement, production, and quality departments. Using only the engineering, marketing, and finance departments can be harmful due to inadequate knowledge of the subcontracts base, production, and quality technology lead-times and acquisition of people skills.

Operating Plan

Does the company have an adequate yearly operating plan that is laid out with quarterly objectives? The objectives should be specific in the sales, the operating costs, the pretax generation of funds, the return on equity/return on investment, and the capital expenditures needed to accomplish the sales volume and expected profit return. The objectives that are defined in the operating plan should be definitive enough to challenge the functional departments. Figure 3 shows a structure that could be used to trace the completeness of the objectives and the strategic and operating plan.

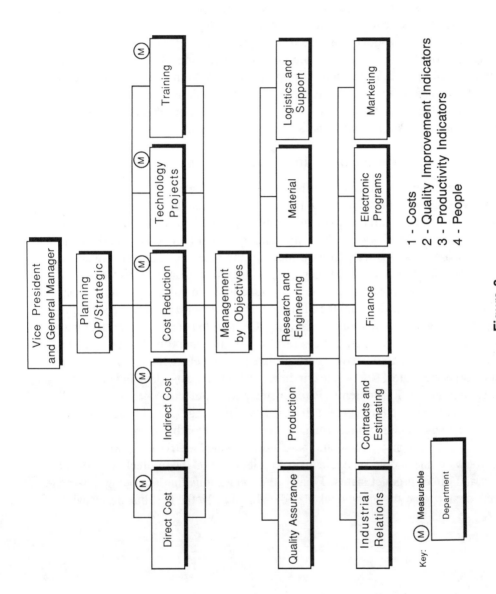

Figure 3
Departmental Structure

Objectives Program

Does the company have a MBO program that is definitive and attainable, and that reaches the functional departments? The objectives should address the critical accomplishments needed to fulfill the strategic and operating plans. They should address the direct and indirect costs, and the quality and productivity improvements that will meet the cost reduction goals. Examples of categories are value engineering, productivity, suggestions, management improvement, etc. Each line director or manager should have at least six and not more than nine MBOs, time-phased over the operating year. They should be agreed to by both the vice president and the line department manager. These should form the basis for the annual performance appraisal and compensation reviews. Figure 4 shows one company's format. There are many books, formats, and systems readily available on the market.

Management Information System

Does the organization have a well-developed, automated MIS? As discussed previously, a manager must have data for real-time use and historical comparison to set standards. In a small company or organization, perhaps this can be handled intuitively by a real hands-on, stick-to-the-knitting type of individual. But the large majority of organizations have to have meat on the bones to efficiently manage. The MIS should start with the strategic plan, operating plan, objectives for the organization and the objectives for the major functional departments. The number of indicators can vary widely, but the MIS should track downward from the strategic, operations and objectives to profit, cash flow, ROE/ROI to people — hire/loss rates, awards, special recognition, employees service — to the operations functions. The operating functions should have overtime use, absenteeism rates (salaried and hourly), grievance rates, safety rates, indirect and direct costs, data and computer budgets, and the top 10 problems (Pareto principle). The "customer is supreme" aspect should be covered in regular scheduled staff meetings, monthly supervisory council meetings, quarterly performance reviews, and monthly program reviews. Additionally, the organization should have a documented matrix of customers and key individuals and should schedule visits to brief them on the indirect operational aspects and direct product status. Finally, the innovations that are being worked with the organization should be tracked and highlighted by the first line performers.

INDIVIDUAL OBJECTIVES
FOR 19___
Page x of x

Title of Participant's Position

INSTRUCTIONS: Each objective, and at year end the brief supporting statement, is to be stated, whenever possible, in terms of sales, earnings, capture of new business, reduced overhead, numerically increased productivity, improved organizational effectiveness, etc.

① STATEMENT OF OBJECTIVE:

Target: Actual:
Date of Accomplishment

② STATEMENT OF OBJECTIVE:

Target: Actual:
Date of Accomplishment

③ STATEMENT OF OBJECTIVE:

Target: Actual:
Date of Accomplishment

④ STATEMENT OF OBJECTIVE:

Target: Actual:
Date of Accomplishment

YEAR'S PERFORMANCE RESULTED IN CONTRIBUTIONS TO: (Check one or more as applicable) ☐Earnings ☐Growth ☐Return on investment ☐Other
SUPPORTING STATEMENT:

_____
Participant's Supervisor's Signature and Date

_____
Participant's Signature and Date

_____
Type Participant's Name

Figure 4
Individual Objectives

Product Quality Improvement Program

Does the organization have a formal quality improvement program (QIP) with aggressive, but attainable, improvement goals? U.S. industry must drastically improve product quality — service software and hardware — and reduce manufacturing costs to compete within the world marketplace. The QIP has to address both white-collar and blue-collar tasks. One anonymous source recently stated, "In a recent study made by a corporate quality and productivity council, it was discovered that 27 percent of all failure costs were due to 'support personnel rework' as opposed to only 9 percent due to 'hands-on personnel rework'! Put simply, this says that management and professionals are responsible for 67 percent more failure costs than hourly personnel."

In response to the DOD's "Bottom Line I" conference, held at Fort McNair, Washington, DC, in May 1982, General Dynamics Corporation — the number one DOD contractor with $5.9 billion in sales in 1982 — established a formal corporate QIP.[11] The thrust of the program was to improve quality and reduce costs in every organization. Thirteen common corporate parameters (Figure 5) were set with stringent performance parameters — most as high as 20 to 30 percent over a baseline period of actuals. The program was initially established in September 1982 in eight major functional departments:

- Research and Engineering
- Production
- Electronic Fabrication Center
- Quality Assurance
- Materials/Procurement
- Logistics
- F-16 Program Office
- Computer Data Center

Added in 1983 were:

- Finance/Controller
- Industrial Relations
- Contracts and Estimating

Quality Improvement Program

Parameters	Baseline Measure 1981 Average	1984		1985 Goal
		Goal	Dec Cumulative Achieved	
• Scrap (Labor) as a percent of direct labor hours	.61%	.27%	.35%	.27%
• Scrap (Material) as a percent of issues	2.00%	.90%	1.11%	.88%
• Rework and Repair as a percent of direct labor hours	2.38%	1.60%	1.73%	1.40%
• Total Scrap and Rework Reduction as a percent of 1981 average	X	X	X	X
• First Time Yield	66.2%	85.0%	82.2%	86.0%
• Inspection Escapes	18.7%	12.7%	12.8%	8.7%
• Number of QARs per 1,000 direct labor hours	4.39	2.46	2.60	2.21
• On-Time Delivery of Material Requirements	97.32%	97.35%	97.2%	97.46%
• Accepted Purchased Items	93.82%	95.84%	95.4%	95.12%
• Changes Per Drawing	35%	25.8%	19.9%	18.2%
• Software Change Requests	––	––	––	––
• Deviations/Waivers	40.0	62.0*	28.2	44.0
• Service Report Response Time	45.7%	70.0%	70.1%	73.0%
• Total Division Overtime as a percent of total straight time hours	6.4%	5%	5.1%	5%

* Year-End. 25 at Mid-Year

Figure 5
Quality Improvement Program

The program was designed for total product quality. The policy is to improve systems and processes prior to design release, material acquisition, fabrication, and assembly to assure that quality is built-in, rather than attempting to inspect and test quality into the end products. The three main features of the QIP approach are top level management commitment, annual improvement goals that are measured and reported, and a massive training and awareness program.

Product quality is affected by all these — the "make it work" engineering changes, shortages on the line, out-of-station installations, low first time yields, repairs, poor reliability in the field, slow and inaccurate data systems, equipments delivered with waivers or deviations, and excessive overtime usage. General Dynamics initially tried to isolate those factors where they could capture the larger near time benefits. They are expanding the program more into the white-collar areas through the QIP and productivity programs.

Supervisory Selection Board

The product always resembles the supervisor. It would, therefore, seem prudent to qualify supervisors for their leadership qualities along with their technical know-how. Supervisors have many of the powers contained in the Taft Hartley Law — the power to "hire, fire, suspend, promote, demote, or effectively recommend." This power cannot be handed out lightly, and it will have to be given to those who have demonstrated mature competence in the skills of supervision. Although technical know-how is important, it is only one third of the triad of technical, interpersonal, and administrative skills.[12] Considering the fact that time and effort expended in selecting supervisors has a substantial return on investment, the following method is suggested for the engineering, manufacturing, quality, subcontracts, logistics departments, and other departments[13]:

1. A supervisory selection board should be established to review and select candidates considered qualified and who are nominated by the organization heads.
2. The board should consist of:
   - Industrial relations (with employee dossier).
   - Engineering.
   - Manufacturing engineering.
   - Quality assurance.
   - A qualified psychologist (to listen during interviews).
3. The sequence of events should consist of:
   - Reviewing candidate desires.
   - Screening out those with unfavorable histories.
   - Selecting candidates.
   - Interviewing candidates:
     — Can they read and understand engineering documentation (engineer member)?
     — Are they familiar with planning and bills of materials (manufacturing member)?

— How would they go about supervising people (industrial relations member)?
— How would they handle problem employees (industrial relations member)?
— What is the understanding of union or company procedures (industrial relations member)?
— What is their understanding and attitude about quality requirements (quality member)?

General Management of Business Functions

The overall financial management and control of a corporation is a composite of judgments exercised by companies. Any well-structured organization will have policies that establish the scope and limitations of authority possessed by each management element. The chief operating official, general manager, and/or department head should state the policies, objectives, and assignments of authorities and responsibilities to subordinate managers via a formalized system. This documentation forms a management system whereby the company carries out its business commitments. It is expected that the company would have an internal audit system to ensure that authority is not exceeded and that the proper fiduciaries are carried out. The implementation of higher echelon decisions and much of the authority for committing the company's resources is vested with middle management. A well-operated company has a system for executive evaluation of middle management stewardship.

Contract and Sales Order Requirements

Does the company have a system for analyzing contracts and sales orders and assigning responsibility for fulfilling these requirements? The standard procedures should address the dollar value for sales and procurement engagements by those authorized. A composite from several companies' policies could be:

- General Manager — $1 million to $2 million depending on the size of the company and whether the corporation operates on a centralized ($1 million to $5 million) or decentralized ($5 million to $25 million) concept.
- Contracts Vice President — Same authority as general manager.
- Program Director — Usually one half of that assigned the general manager.
- Finance Vice President — Same authority as general manager.
- Materials Vice President — For placement of purchasing and subcontracts, the values should be approximately one half the general manager's.
- Plant Services — $25,000 to $100,000 for outside subcontracted maintenance and construction.

Internal Audit System

Does the company have an internal audit system to ensure that financial authorities are exercised within prescribed limitations and good business practices? Industry and educational organizations that do business with the federal government either as a prime contractor or subcontractor must expect preaward and postaward audits of proposals, actual costs, overhead, and even management systems.[14] These audits are done by the General Accounting Office, Defense Contract Audit Agency, Defense Contract Administration Service, or one of the Army, Air Force, or Navy Plant Representative Offices. The topics range from A to Z and some examples that an internal audit group should review are listed as follows:

- Adequacy of cost accounting system.
- Engineering change cost.
- Labor productivity.
- Incurred costs and vendor quotations.
- Pricing inventory items.
- Pyramiding of costs and rights on purchased material.
- Make-or-buy decisions.
- Scrap, spoilage, rework, obsolescence, and inventory adjustments.
- Allocation bases.
- Types of overhead rates.
- Travel and subsistence, etc.
- Product audit.
- Overtime control.
- Facilities usage.
- Tooling control and accountability.
- Security.
- Computer usage.
- Employee compensation.

Significant Financial Commitments

Is there a system for reporting all significant financial management decisions to the executive levels? This system, combined with a good internal audit crosscheck, is required to make sure that no one is "cooking the books." Stories of accounting irregularities are familiar tales, usually telling how top management inflated profits or how some low-level employee absconded with corporate funds. But recently, to meet profit goals, boost bonuses, etc., many middle managers fudge the numbers to fool the boss. They weren't stealing money or taking bribes, kickbacks, or anything like that. Rather they were cooking the books — changing some of the performance measurement figures, the quality improvement statistics, etc. — to keep their jobs or improve their chances of advancement. This is a whole new trend of disclosing fraud. The fraud has been so large at some companies that the companies were required to restate their financial results. One company's audit committee's recommendations were published as a textbook on internal controls, spelling out the personnel and policies needed to do an effective job.[15] These reports can be indicators of totals, but they need thresholds for larger transactions; e.g., on the receivables report, the larger ones should be itemized above a certain dollar limit ($100,000 to $250,000 depending on the size of the company).

Manpower Requirements

Is there a system that identifies how the company and department determines and implements manpower requirements and uses the manpower to satisfy present or projected business (contractual) commitments? Some type of estimating methodology is needed to track both direct and indirect costs. Ratios can be used as indicators between indirect and direct, and these should be converted into manpower targets that should be tracked on a quarterly basis. If the direct manpower is to be reduced by a target percentage, then the indirect members should go down also. In today's world of technology, computers, and more service-oriented paperwork tasks, it is crucial that the indirect allocation and classifications be watched very closely. If four machine operators are replaced by numerical control machines, then the computer programmers should be direct, not indirect as the old rules have stipulated.

General Management of Technical Functions

The quality program covers all of the company's managerial elements related to the design, development, manufacture, delivery, and field support of a product within cost, on schedule, meeting contract specifications, and satisfying the customer. Because a quality program is not the sole responsibility of any single company organization, the company must identify the organizations and functions responsible for implementing and maintaining an effective quality program. It is essential that all quality requirements are assigned to the functional organizations in consonance with the stated objectives of the company. Quality assurance or product assurance starts at the top; management policies and actions are the determining factors in a company's success. Figure 6 shows how General Dynamics responds to the policy requirements of MIL-Q-9858A.(Department of Defense Specification on a Total Quality Program.)

GENERAL DYNAMICS

EXECUTIVE MEMORANDUM
No. 81-2
4 February 1981

To: Division General Managers, Subsidiary Presidents, and Corporate Directors of Quality Assurance

Subject: Quality Assurance Responsibility

1. It is General Dynamics' policy to provide quality products and services commensurate with the standards demanded by our customers. It is the Division General Manager's responsibility to establish and maintain sound,cost-effective quality practices in his division.

2. Each General Manager will be held accountable for obtaining the requisite quality and for insuring that proper actions are taken in engineering, manufacturing, materials, and quality assurance. All other functions also share in the responsibilty to deliver quality products and services.

3. General Dynamics recognizes the vital importance of its product and services in our national economy and defense and that of our foreign customers. This policy will not be compromised.

O. C. Boileau
President

Figure 6
General Dynamics Corporate Quality Policy

Part Two

Product Assurance Organization

Does the company have a product assurance organization that will act for the general manager and implement a total quality program? Some organizations do not have a definitive quality department reporting to the top company official; neither do they have a grasp of what total quality is. Some companies are still laboring under the quality inspection syndrome; that is, quality is a part of production or worse yet, a part of fabrication, which basically inspects fabrication and assembly. A total quality program department could be aligned as shown in Figure 7.

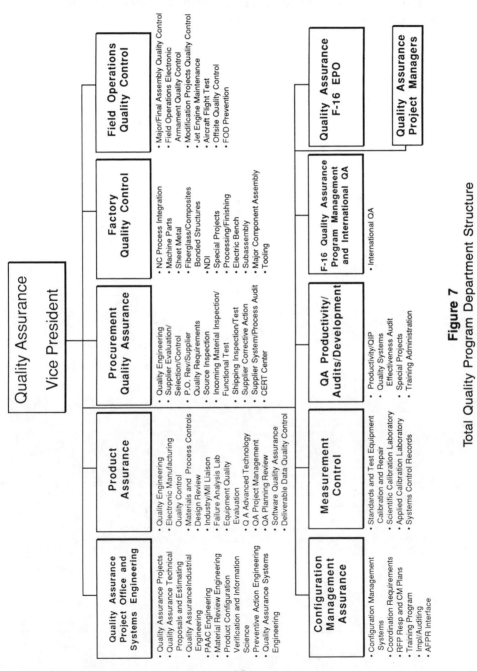

Figure 7
Total Quality Program Department Structure

29

Quality Contractual Requirements

Has the company identified all quality program contractual requirements and assigned authority and responsibility for their accomplishment? Most organizations do this by a review of the proposed contract (request for proposal) and break out the tasks for bidding by all functional areas. If and when the contract or work authorization is received, then the sectionized statements of work and budgets are passed out by either a program office (if used in the company) or the finance department. In other instances, the procedures are documented and laid out for most complex procurements and are handled over and over again. Figure 8 shows a sample of the standard practices and the assignees' responsibilities.

Subject	Data Systems Division	Electronic Products	Public Affairs	Industrial Relations	Productivity	General Counsel — Legal	F-16 Internat Prog. Office	F-16XL Program Office	Special Projects	Contracts and Estimating	Quality Assurance	Marketing	Industrial Engineering	Plant Services	Manufacturing Development	Prod. Planning and Control	Tooling and MSE	Manufacturing	F-16 Production Management	Production	Logistics and Support	F-111 Program Office	Finance	Material	Research and Engineering	F-16 Program Office	GD/FW Top Management	GD Corporate Office	Customer/Air Force
Quality Assurance Section 9																													
Service Reports/Material Deficiency Reports		X						X		X	X			X		X		X			X	X		X	X	X			X
GFAE/GFP Material Deficiency Report Exhibits										X	X			X		X					X			X					X
Control of Nonconforming Material											X		X			X	X	X							X				X
Expanded QAR Coverage - Manufacturing Corrections	X	X									X		X			X		X							X				
Standard Repair/Standard Disposition											X			X	X	X		X						X	X				X
Material Survey											X									X	X	X		X	X	X	X		X
Quality Assurance Audits											X		X			X	X	X						X	X	X	X		X
One Time Inspection - F-16											X					X	X	X			X				X	X			X
Discrepancy Document Processing for Flight Line Aircraft								X			X		X					X											X
Quality Cost Reporting											X					X		X					X		X				
Control of Dispositioned Hardware - Static and Durability Articles											X											X		X	X	X	X		
Quality Assurance of Research and Engineering Deliverable Software	X	X									X						X							X	X	X	X		
Verification of Software Used as a Medium of Inspection	X																								X	X			

Figure 8

Standard Practices Impact on Specific Organizations

Quality Status

Does the company require some managerial organization to review the status and adequacy of the quality program and track the required corrective action? This is one of the hardest parts of the total quality program, and it is handled poorly by most companies. Quality should be the assigned goal of all organizations as delineated by the policy letter at General Dynamics Fort Worth division (Figure 9).

GENERAL DYNAMICS   7 January 1987
Fort Worth Division

DIVISION NOTICE NO. 87-1

To: All Supervision

Subject: Quality Assurance Policy and Responsibilities

General Dynamics' policy regarding Quality Assurance is delineated in the O.C. Boileau Executive Memorandum attached.

Responsibility for obtaining product quality rests with specific functional organizations, e.g. Research & Engineering, for design quality, Material, for the quality of purchased items, and Manufacturing, for production quality.

Final acceptance of our products to prescribed quality standards is the assigned responsibility of Quality Assurance. This latter assignment does not relieve other organizations of their more direct and immediate responsibilities of designing, purchasing, and building quality into Fort Worth products.

continued personal commitment and support of every member of our management team to ensure that continuing excellent product quality is achieved.

Charles A. Anderson
Vice President & General Manager

Figure 9
General Dynamics Fort Worth Division Quality Policy

Also, a product assurance/quality organization should be on equal footing with engineering, production, finance, contracts, etc., and report to the general manager. The product assurance/quality assurance department should have the charter to review and provide appropriate quality assurance parts of Request for Proposal (RFP)/Request for Quotes (RFQ) responses. They should also review all contracts for the appropriate inspection criteria. The product assurance/quality assurance department should have the charter and be expected to audit all organizations to determine how well product quality is being affected. This gambit goes from the design departments through the field service departments. Does your company have an inspection department, a quality control department, or the ultimate, a product assurance/quality assurance department?

THREE

Functional Excellence

"There is nothing more wasteful than
doing efficiently that which is not
necessary."

Sir Royce

Executives tend to latch on to any managerial idea that offers a quick fix. A company's culture — its shared values, beliefs, and rituals — strongly influences its success or failure. While the trek through the past four decades has offered a plethora of good concepts, none or all of them may work in the company, division, or department.

The list of ideas covers the full range from Theory X to Theory Y to Theory Z. MBOs from the 1950s, Zero Defects from the 1960s, Zero-Based Budgeting from the 1970s, and One-Minute Managing and Management-by-Walking-Around from the 1980s are all still useful. By taking a look at yourself, you can determine the cultural differences and see which concepts work best in achieving functional excellence. You have to plan and develop strategies and master schedules; but total success depends on merging them together with sincere commitment from top management, or they will be doomed to failure.

Perform a continual management assessment program, relentlessly push the techniques that will work for your company, division, or department, and push, push!

Quality Assurance

"Quality is never an accident; it is
always the result of intelligent effort."

John Ruskin

Improving the profit position of a company requires continuous ingenuity and innovation. A healthy company or department functions better and allows the best use of capital; it is more efficient in terms of quantity and quality of output and is predictable. Just like a scheduled physical examination, periodically every firm should have a self-examination. This examination or MAP should look at the organization, the procedures, and instructions as they relate to hardware, software, and services.

Organizational Freedom

Does the quality assurance vice president, director, or manager have the authority and organizational freedom to exercise top managements' dictates? Quality has to be independent to fully evaluate the total organization of engineering, production, logistics, finance, procurement, etc. The following points should be important to any company:

- The quality assurance manager should be recognized as one of the high-level decision makers in the top structure.
- Quality should be more than just inspection; it should have engineering personnel who can relate to the design and production engineers.
- Quality control must have and give final acceptance based on sound, hard facts and not on individual opinion.
- The quality function must be independent of manufacturing and report to upper management to qualify for DOD and NASA contracts.[16]

Procedural Guidance

Does the quality organization have the necessary procedures for quality program responsibilities assigned by company management policies? (See MIL-Q-9858A, MIL-STD-1520, MIL-STD-1535, and MIL-STD-52779A.) Policies, procedures, plans, and guidance are necessary if the company or department is to turn out consistent work. Traditionally, most companies have a quality manual that is based on a three-tier system: (1) corporate and division policies, (2) system-level procedures between departments, and (3) quality department instructions. However, when there are multiple programs or new subplants, then the use of program plans could be used to meet regulatory, customer, or unique company specifications. Figure 10 shows a "manual hierarchy" used by Otis Engineering, General Dynamics, Vought, and other companies using matrix organizations. Appendix V of the quality program standard developed under the sponsorship of the American National Standards Institute provides a universally applicable document. The advantages of using this standard are consistency, uniformity, and ease of composing new documents. It also provides an easy "audit" trail for those many reviews and system audits by the various government agencies and customers. Figure 11 is a typical outline of a minimum quality assurance manual. Standardization through a subtier system helps interface quality department manuals and corporate or systems level policies and procedures.[17]

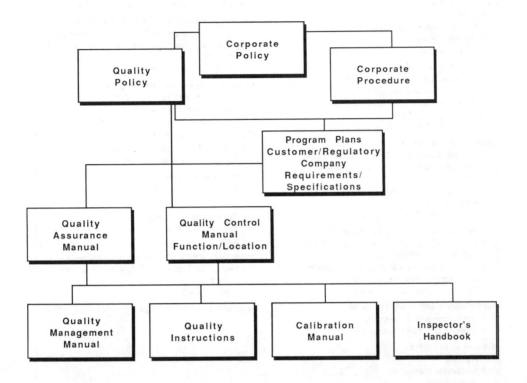

Figure 10
Manual Hierarchy

General:
- Statement of quality assurance policy approved by the principal manager of the facility
- Organization charts
- Control of quality assurance manual

Design control:
- Order entry
- Design control and review
- Design changes
- Design adequacy

Procurement control:
- Purchasing specification control
- Material purchase requisitions
- Source evaluation and qualification
- Receiving inspection
- Nonconforming incoming material

Instructions, procedures, and drawings:
- Control of engineering documents drawings, standards, specifications, and purchase requisitions
- Source evaluation and qualification
- Receiving inspection
- Nonconforming incoming material

Instructions, procedures, and drawings:
- Control of engineering documents drawings, standards, specifications, and procedures
- Control of revisions to drawings, standards, specifications, and procedures
- Traveler or process sheet system

Identification and control of items:
- Overall traceability program
- Material identification program

Control of processes:
- Welding
- Nondestructive testing
- Heat treating
- Machining, assembling, and others

Inspection:
- Inspection program
- Qualification of quality control personnel

Test control:
- Performance testing
- Function testing
- Other required finished product testing

Control of measuring and test equipment:
- Control of gauges and measuring equipment
- Required action when discrepant equipment is detected
- Gauge usage control

Inspection, test, and operating status:
- Control of finished equipment
- Identification of equipment
- Handling storage and shipping instructions

Nonconformance control:
- Control of nonconforming material
- Significant condition corrective action

Quality assurance records:
- Quality assurance records
- Record storage

Quality assurance audits:
- Internal audit program
- Corrective action system

Equipment failure and malfunction analysis:
- Method for processing failure and malfunction reports
- Corrective action

Appendix (May include copies of referenced forms)

Figure 11
Typical Outline of a Minimum Quality Assurance Manual

Quality Feedback

Do the quality organization documented procedures clearly define the method of feedback of information within the quality assurance department and between other organizations? Once you have determined that you have the quality program and procedures in question, it is time to give the system a fitness check. Some warning signs are frequent customer complaints, recurring manufacturing delinquencies, frequent shortages of materials, regular use of nonconforming materials, high quality costs, and poor employee attitudes.[18] This checklist (Figure 12) will check your total quality system and will allow you to detect, diagnose, and treat areas before they need "major surgery." Take the time and corrective action for a healthy company or department.

Fitness Checklist

To determine the state of the company's quality health, fill out the checklist. Answer the questions as objectively and completely as possible using the following point system:
- I'm satisfied with the way we handle this issue. It is not a problem at our company. (4 points)
- This issue is being addressed, but we need improvement in this area. (3 points)
- We do take this into consideration, but it is handled poorly. We definitely need improvement in this area. (2 points)
- I feel this is a problem area in our company. Either we do not address this issue or do so very poorly. (1 point)

Warning signs and associated issues or problems

I. Frequent customer complaints

_____ 1. Is there a system to monitor complaints?
_____ 2. Is there a formal program to investigate customer complaints?
_____ 3. Are the above responsibilities assigned to individuals?
_____ 4. Are any adverse trends apparent in the number and severity of customer returns?
_____ 5. Is analysis being performed to identify any patterns?
_____ 6. Can you categorize the complaints as design, conformance, or nonquality related?
_____ 7. Are complaints being reviewed with engineering, R&D, inspectors, foremen, etc.?

II. Recurring problems

_____ 8. Is there a formal system to address in-house problems?
_____ 9. Do representatives from the various departments involved contribute to the solution of quality problems?
_____ 10. Are status reports issued regarding efforts to eliminate these problems?
_____ 11. If most problems associated with a particular product or process are design-related, are changes or improvements being sought?
_____ 12. Is there at least one individual that is an expert at troublshooting problems?

III. Management input required for acceptance

_____ 13. Do you have a formal material review board (MRB) system?
_____ 14. Do a high percentage of product or component inspections result in MRB decisions?

_____ 15. Are you taking aciton if the same items appear week after week?
_____ 16. After MRB meetings, is corrective action being initiated in a formal manner?
_____ 17. Are MRB decisions often inconclusive? Do they require decisions by higher management?

IV. Frequent shortages of material

_____ 18. Are operators or production lines often idle because of material shortages due to quality problems?
_____ 19. Are shipments to customers delayed because of quality problems?
_____ 20. Does the production control department have difficulty scheduling because of numerous rejections?
_____ 21. Do you have excess work-in-process because of high reject rates?
_____ 22. Do you have a glut of excess material when things are running well?

V. Regular use of nonconforming materials

_____ 23. Do you have a high percentage of use-as-is MRB decisions?
_____ 24. Is a specification change initiated after several use-as-is decisions for the same problem?
_____ 25. Do you have a formal system to review new product specifications after production experience has been gained?
_____ 26. Do you have a procedure to determine what the real requirements are for items that were rejected but later used without apparent difficulties?
_____ 27. When you use nonconforming materials are you certain that the customer will not be receiving an inferior product?

VI. New products

_____ 28. Do you have a product assurance review or other means of formal quality planning?
_____ 29. Do you perform process capability studies before actual production begins?
_____ 30. Are product specifications in line with your process capabilities?
_____ 31. Are operators and inspectors briefed on the new product's characteristics, requirements, and peculiarities?
_____ 32. Is there a clear understanding between you and your customer about product specifications and expectations?

Figure 12
Quality Fitness Checklist

VII. Quality costs

_____ 33. Does the company issue a formal quality cost report periodically?

_____ 34. Are all costs associated with the quality function properly identified and accounted for?

_____ 35. Are quality costs hidden in standards or in other manufacturing costs?

_____ 36. Are quality cost improvements incorporated into departmental goals (other than the QC department)?

_____ 37. Does management feel the quality cost report is accurate and a valuable management aid?

_____ 38. If unfavorable trends appear in the quality cost report, does management investigate?

VIII. Poor employee attitude

_____ 39. Does someone explain to each worker exactly what is expected in his or her job?

_____ 40. Is there a plan of close cooperation for the purpose of improving quality involving supervisors of departments that supply or receive components from one another?

_____ 41. When work is rejected, are the workers concerned, and made aware of what is wrong and what they can do to improve?

_____ 42. Is each department provided with a list of defective work that they produced in a given week or month so that actions can be taken to prevent recurrence?

_____ 43. As a professional concerned with quality do you set aside a definite amount of time for actual inspection of product going through the plant?

_____ 44. Do you have a system for getting suggestions from your workers on how to improve quality?

_____ 45. Are regular talks held with each worker regarding the quality of the work he or she is doing?

_____ 46. Are workers aware of the cost of defective work in their departments?

_____ 47. Are examples of good and bad work displayed for workers to observe?

_____ 48. Do you have any method for arousing pride in workmanship?

_____ 49. Is each worker acquainted with the relationship between quality workmanship and job security?

_____ 50. Do employees understand the value placed on quality performance when they are considered for raises or promotions?

Total the number of points from all the questions and compare the total of the table. The diagnosis should help toward a quality fitness program. The checklist may be filled out by managers of departments other than the quality control or assurance departments. Section VIII, which deals with employee attitudes, would provide useful information if filled out by a sampling of hourly personnel. Early detection and appropriate corrective action are the best defenses against more serious problems.

Survey results analysis	
Point total	**Diagnosis**
180-200	Excellent. If there were an Olympics for quality, you'd be fit enough to enter!
160-179	Good. With a little more effort and discipline, you can be a winner.
135-159	Fair. You need some concentrated effort to get in shape, but there is still hope.
100-134	Poor. It will take treatment from specialists to pull you through.
99 or less	Terminal. Unless major surgery is undertaken immediately, there is little hope for you.

Figure 12 (cont.)
Quality Fitness Checklist

Quality Costs

Do the company's procedures provide for collection and use of total quality costs data as a part of managing the quality assurance program? The real value of a quality program is ultimately determined by its ability to contribute to customer satisfaction and profits. To understand the concept of quality costs, you must have a clear picture of the difference between quality costs and the cost of running the quality department! Figure 13 lists some of the costs that should be in the cost evaluation system of poor quality.[19]

Please use the matrix below to indicate which quality cost elements your company monitors and how it categorizes each element. Some elements cover a broad range of activities. Please check as many categories as appropriate for each element (P=prevention, A=appraisal, IF=internal failure, EF=external failure, F=failure (not broken down into internal and external failures, and NM=not measured by company's quality cost system).

	P	A	IF	EF	F	NM
Quality data acquisition and analysis						
Administrative costs						
Product review						
Process control						
Quality engineering						
Quality planning by functions other than quality						
Training to improve quality						
Inspection and test						
Field evaluation and testing						
Inspection and test set-up						
Quality audits						
Maintenance/calibration test/inspection equip.						
Maintenance/calibration production equipment						
Scrap						
Rework and repair						
Downtime						
Troubleshooting or failure analysis						
Reinspect or retest						
Scrap and rework--fault of vendor						
Downgrading						
Complaints						
Product or customer service						
Products rejected and returned						
Returned material repair						
Discrepant material activity						
Warranty charges						
Marketing error						
Engineering error						
Factory or installation error						
Recalls						
Product liability						

Figure 13
Quality Cost Elements

In short, any cost that would not have been expended if quality work was perfect contributes to the cost of quality. This listing is not all inclusive; the indirect or white-collar departments need to be carefully looked at for the input to inefficiencies and quality cost: excessive hiring times, error rates or personnel medical payments, errors in finance journal entries, wrong reservations in travel, etc.

Once you have the system laid out, to whom does the "cost" data go? If it is not given a dollar value and indexed to sales base, cost base, labor base, unit base, etc., then it is difficult to show management the data. The report should be used by most of the senior staff (i.e., general manager, vice president of operations, vice president of finance, and vice president of programs). Figure 14 shows two reports that Fairchild used in the quality program.[20] Perhaps the most revealing is a chart depicting the percentage profit lost if the cost of quality had been near zero. Percentages of 2 to 10 percent should be of major concern to top management. Productivity is quality in quantity!

Farmingdale

Month August 1978

CODE	Element Description	Program (In Thousands)					Total All Programs
		A-10	SSVT	F-4	747	Misc	
K	Material Review Activity	71.8	—	.7	7.7	—	80.2
L	Corrective Action	249.8	—	.9	2.7	—	253.4
X	Troubleshooting/Failure Analysis	47.2	—	—	.8	—	48.0
R	Rework/Repair	128.6	.4	6.3	26.1	—	161.4
P	Scrap	19.2	—	—	0.5	—	19.7
V	RWK/RPR/Scrap — Vendor Resp.	27.1	—	.1	2.6	—	29.8
U	Processing of Customer Complaints	5.4	—	—	1.4	—	6.8
I	Processing of Customer Ret'n'd Mat'l	23.3	—	—	—	—	23.3
J	Field Services	—	—	—	—	—	—
Y	Warranty Costs	.1	—	—	—	—	.1
	Total "Unquality" Costs	572.5	.4	8.0	41.8	—	622.7
	Quality Prevention and Appraisal	718.2	.9	8.3	69.8	38.6	835.8
	Total Quality Costs	1290.7	1.3	16.3	111.6	38.6	1458.5
	MFG Direct Labor Costs	6973.8	7.5	116.5	882.8	396.5	8377.1
	Scrap/Rework/Repair as % of MFG D/L	2.1	5.3	5.4	3.0	—	2.2
	Cost Input	20943.4	66.1	978.4	1946.6	104.1	24038.6
	Total Quality Costs as % of Cost Input	6.2	2.0	1.7	5.7	37.1	6.1

Quality Costs by Program

Figure 14
Quality Cost by Program and Element

QUALITY COST REPORT
For the month ending _____

(In Thousands of U. S. Dollars)

Description	Current Month			Year to Date		
	Quality Costs	As a Percent of		Quality Costs	As a Percent of	
		Sales	Other		Sales	Other
1 Prevention Costs						
1.1 Product Design						
1.2 Purchasing						
1.3 Quality Planning						
1.4 Quality Administration						
1.5 Quality Training						
1.6 Quality Audits						
Total Prevention Costs						
Prevention Targets						
2 Appraisal Costs						
2.1 Product Qualification Tests						
2.2 Supplier Production Inspection and Test						
2.3 In Process and Final Inspection and Test						
2.4 Maintenance and Calibration						
Total Appraisal Costs						
Appraisal Targets						
3 Failure Costs						
3.1 Design Failure Costs						
3.2 Supplier Product Rejects						
3.3 Material Review and Corrective Action						
3.4 Rework						
3.5 Scrap						
3.6 External Failure Costs						
Total Failure Costs						
Failure Targets						
Total Quality Costs						
Total Quality Targets						

Memo Data	Current Month		Year to Date		Full Year	
	Budget	Actual	Budget	Actual	Budget	Actual
Net Sales						
Other Base (Specify)						

Quality Costs by Element

Figure 14 (cont.)
Quality Cost by Program and Element

Discrepancy Detection

Does the company's quality system allow detection of discrepancies and ensure that timely and positive corrective action is taken to eliminate the cause? There are problems in any manufacturing or service operation. It is imperative that the corrective action system includes as a minimum: (1) analysis of data and examination of products scrapped or reworked to determine extent and cause, (2) analysis of trends in processed or performance work to prevent nonconforming products, and (3) introduction of required improvements and corrections, an initial review of the adequacy of such measures, and monitoring of the effectiveness of the corrective action taken. These areas of corrective action and use of quality cost data are probably the two most neglected areas in a company's quality program. I will repeat many times in this book that a company or department will only be successful if a good data system exists and the manager is willing to work hard and be innovative. Corrective action starts with "Paretorizing" the causes for the defects. Take the top 20, 10, or five based on cost consequences, repetition, or chronic shortage issues, then apply the diagnosis and fix-it solution. This type of system should start at the critical suppliers' plants through receiving inspection, assembly, shipping, and field performance. One element of the DOD MIL-STD-1520 should be mentioned specifically and that is a corrective action board. Senior management from engineering, production, quality, material/procurement, and logistics/field service should meet periodically in joint session to discuss those onerous problems to which a vice president or director can utter the right words and move mountains. The agenda is published prior to the meeting and people specifically are called in to give the causes and suggest solutions.

Calibration System

Does the company have an effective metrology and calibration system for standards, measuring, and test equipment? (See MIL-Q-9858A, MIL-I-45208, MIL-STD-45662, and NHB 5300.4[1b].) The company should provide and maintain gauges and other measuring and testing devices necessary to ensure that hardware, software, and services conform to technical requirements. The objective of the system is to ensure that inspection and test equipment is adjusted, replaced, or repaired before it becomes inaccurate. The system should consist of:

- Labels, tags, color codes, forms, and a requirement for calibration procedures.
- Certified primary company or reference standards traceable to the National Bureau of Standards.
- Listings by department of calibration status and delinquents. There should be a low limit on the number of tools and instruments that can be out of calibration.
- Personally owned tools should be in the system and calibrated, especially if used for inspection.
- The inspection department should have calibration as an inspection check, before "buying" off on items.

Procurement Quality Assurance

Does the company have adequate control over the quality of purchased materials and products? The quality assurance and material/procurement departments have to select good suppliers based on technical, quality manufacturing, delivery schedules, and cost parameters. Both a mix of source inspection and receiving inspection has to be used based on criticality and quantities of the products. Tracking of source-inspected, receiving-inspected government furnished property is a key to see how the materials perform as they are assembled and tested during the complete flow-through to end-item acceptance. Removal rates of as high as 150 percent have been seen at some DOD aircraft and missile manufacturers. A high removal rate during the manufacturing flow can be disruptive and cause slowdown of the move rates, out-of-station installations, high overtime usage, and disruption of previously installed hardware.

There are several supplier evaluation systems, but the most effective program starts with top management's insistence that defective material never appear on the receiving dock premises. Some noteworthy company systems are RCA's Certified Vendor Representative program and General Dynamics' Vendor Excellence Designee program. These systems designate the supplier's key personnel to act for the prime contractor, accepting the supplier's products after the suppliers' normal quality acceptance was completed. Benefits accrue to both the supplier — (1) no waiting for the prime's source inspector, (2) preferred repeat business status, and (3) increased cash flow; and the prime contractor — (1) less source inspectors, thus monetary savings, and (2) more emphasis and trust in the supplier's total system, thus better product quality.

General Dynamics Fort Worth division has developed another system to evaluate suppliers: Supplier Performance Evaluation Criteria (SPEC).[21] The system uses several criteria to analyze costs to the quality of the supplier's product:

- Late deliveries and out-of-station installations.
- Producibility studies (if supplier designs).
- Increased quality or subcontract personnel coverage at supplier facility.
- Convening material review boards at supplier facility.
- Monetary withholdings by customers.
- Aircraft removals or replacements.
- Reflights and ground aborts.
- Stock purges and material surveys.
- Supplier-responsible design changes.
- Reinspections and retest.
- Rework and repairs.
- Corrective action and investigations.
- Special audits.

The costs are accumulated, tracked, and fed back to the supplier's top managers on a periodic basis. The two cost parameters tracked are: (1) the cost to General Dynamics Fort Worth division in cost per 1,000 invoices and (2) total cost to General Dynamics Fort Worth division for typical reports (Figure 15).

43

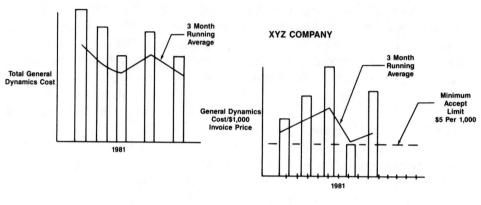

Typical
Report Formats

Cost Element	JAN	FEB	MAR	APR	MAY
1. Out-of-Station Installation	$1,000	$2,000	$6,000	$8,000	$5,000
2. A/C Removal/ Replacements	$ 300	$1,100	$ 700	$ 400	$ 800

Figure 15
Supplier Cost Reports

Part Three

Software Quality

Does the company's quality system provide for an organized approach for the acquisition, development, and maintenance of software products? The software development process has to be proceduralized just like the mechanical or electrical design process. The typical process is shown in Figure 16.[22] If the design process is not proceduralized and followed religiously just as the mechanical and electrical designers do, then the cost will increase significantly (Figure 17). Typical costs can grow from $75 per line of code in the requirements definition area to over $4,000 per line of code to correct it in the system redesign, redevelopment, and retest area. The key software quality checkpoints are listed in Figure 18.

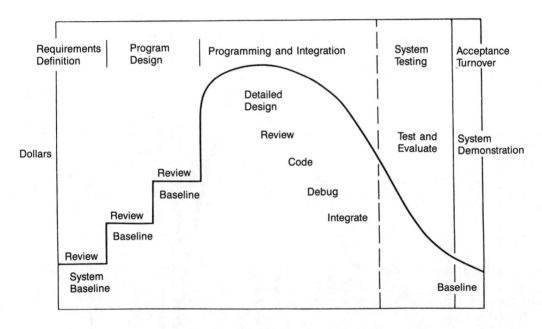

Figure 16
Software Development Process

45

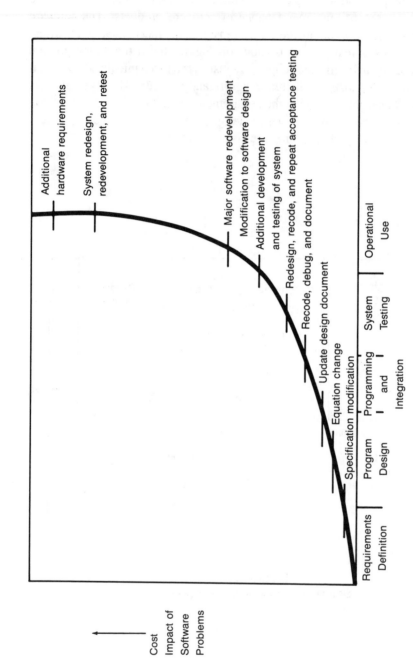

Figure 17
Software Change Cost Impacts

Factors	Development			Evaluation	Post-Development			Expected Cost Saved Cost to Provide
	Requirements Analysis	Design	Code and Debug	System Test	Operation	Revision	Transition	
Correctness	○	○	○	●	●	●		High
Reliability	○	○	○	●	●	●		High
Efficiency	○	○	○		●			Low
Integrity	○	○	○		●			Low
Usability	○	○		●		●		Medium
Maintainability		○	○			●	●	High
Testability		○	○	●		●	●	High
Flexibility		○	○			●	●	Medium
Portability		○	○				●	Medium
Reusability		○	○				●	Medium
Interoperability	○	○		●			●	Low

○ *Where quality factors should be measured*

● *Where impact of poor quality is realized*

Figure 18

Impact of not specifying or Measuring Software Quality Factors

47

Industrial Relations

"Experience is a hard teacher
because she gives the test first,
the lesson afterwards."

Vernon Law

The main objective of the industrial relations department is to develop supportive systems necessary for achieving a goal-oriented organization and managing human resources. The organization may have some of the finest systems for salary administration and promotion of any comparable organization in the country; however, if these fine systems are kept in such secrecy that management does not know how they are applied, you may lose some of your most capable people. Uncertainty of one's future will start one to look for other, greener pastures.

The supportive management systems we are talking about are listed as follows:

- Salary administration systems.
- Reward systems — compensation such as bonuses, profit sharing, and non-financial awards.
- Fringe benefits — pensions, hospitalization, and vacations.
- Employment and staffing.
- Transfers and rotations.
- Labor relations systems.
- Performance reviews.
- Attitude, quality, and other surveys.
- Training and education.
- Information.
- Job enrichment programs.
- Work simplification and work measurement systems.
- Management by objectives and results.

Total System Analysis

Do you review your human resources in total systems terms? This is a system where inputs are gathered from all aspects of the organization. Such an example is shown in Figure 19, where one complete cycle of human resources, planning, performance, and feedback is tracked through the ever-changing environment of an ongoing organization.[23]

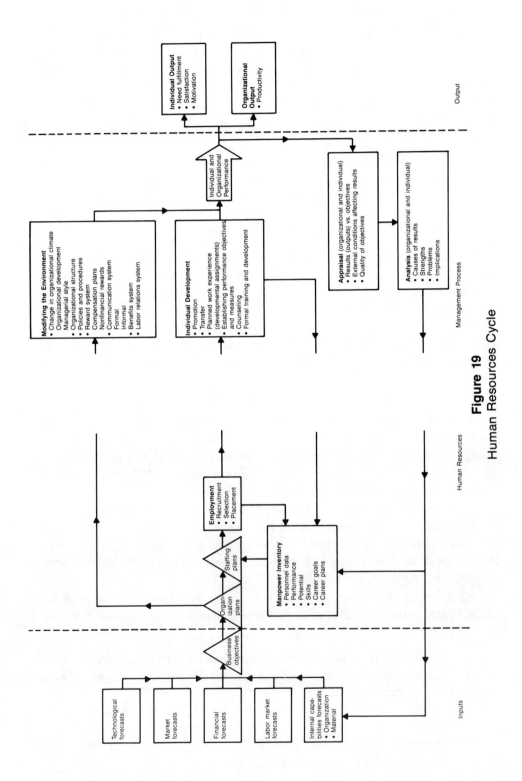

Figure 19
Human Resources Cycle

Management by Objectives Appraisal

Does the company have a MBO appraisal system and do the departments use the results of these for yearly planning? Each division should have a MBO system. Generally, personnel runs this system as part of the appraisal system. The objectives should flow down from the corporate level to the division level to the departments. The key MBOs from the corporate and division levels should reflect the following:

- The percentage of earnings or return on investment for which the company or division should be trying.
- The achievement of significant improvements in the performance objectives of quality, productivity, schedule, and cost. (Note the order of these four objectives; psychologically this is very important.)
- The achievement of new business opportunities or a percentage of market share and the development of new products.

The appraisal system should flow from the key MBOs and show what developments can be made by the individual departments, groups, and sections to help the company run more efficiently. These developments include: scrap, rework, and repair, inventory losses, avoidable engineering changes, field returns, percent acceptable manufactured parts, acceptable percentage of supplier parts, union grievances, overtime, out-of-sequence assembly operations, standard hour efficiency, billing error rates, hiring losses, medical claims per employee, accident rates, etc.

Training Program

Does the company have an effective training program? A complete successful training program should address (1) new hires, (2) technical courses, (3) supervisory training for new supervisors and additional training for those who have been supervisors for more than five years, and (4) management training for those in the second through higher level of management.

The first-line supervisors — the men and women in the middle — face a stiff challenge in the 1980s. Middle and top management will be after them to improve productivity, improve quality, and reduce manufacturing costs. Added to this is the change in the mix of people supervised. Now it includes robots and a larger measure of computers and software.

According to *Iron Age* magazine, there is a way to make the point person of today and tomorrow the kind of first-line supervisor that's needed.[24] Its four principal features all involve training:

1. The foreman must be trained to communicate with his or her workers;
2. The foreman's understanding of human behavior and interpersonal relations must be improved.
3. A supervisory board should select new foremen. Selection can no longer be made on a hit-or-miss basis — the job has become too important.
4. Foremen should be trained effectively. Training must extend back up the management ladder all the way to the top.

Nissan USA is one example of a company that is committed to using a better training approach at their new plant in Smyrna, Tennessee. And to accomplish this, they carefully screen new employees. Their supervisory training program (Figure 20) is designed as a compromise between the Japanese and American system and has the advantages of both.[25]

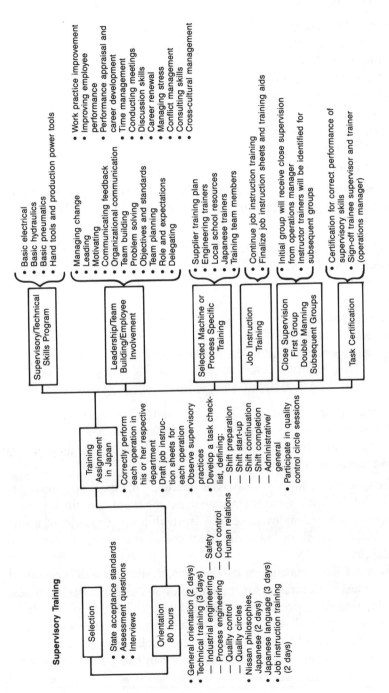

Figure 20
Nissan Training Program

June 5-13, 1983, was designated as Management Week in America by President Reagan and Congress. This was in large part due to the efforts of the National Management Association (NMA). Prior to this in 1980, the NMA took a giant step in setting up the first program to articulate the skills needed by a first-line supervisor. The program provides 140 hours in a modularly sequenced set of courses covering the following areas:

- Introduction to Supervision
- Management Principles
- Communication Skills
- Interpersonal Relationships
- Challenge of a New Employee
- Counseling
- Leadership Development
- Business Concepts
- Law for the Layman

According to Gene Garrett, chairman of the board, NMA, the next step is the Advanced Management Studies Program.[26] The topics in the AMP are listed as follows:

- Building the Person Skill System
- Management Process Skills
- Personal Skills
- Financial Skills
- Professional Development
- Working with Others
- Relating the Operating Unit to the Organization

Hiring Program

Does the company have an effective hiring program? The total hiring program should consider several factors to help line and staff functions meet division standards for effectiveness and efficiency. They should include the following industrial relations performance standards for measuring:

1. Rate of employee turnover per calendar quarter. This indirectly measures the quality of the work place environment and the training of the foremen. Also, the number of employees terminated within three months of hiring is a true quality check of industrial relations' ability to select people for open positions.

2. Timeliness of filling requisitions for hire. If a department puts in a request for hire, it must be necessary. Most companies do this job poorly; politics, staffers delaying the process because of budget decisions, or inaptitude on the industrial relations department's part, are just a few of the reasons lower management becomes frustrated in using the people they need for productivity. Industrial relations should be measured in two parts here: (1) the

time that elapses between the initiating department's release to the formal sign-off by top management; and, (2) the time that industrial relations receives the requisition to the time the new employee walks in the door.

Ask your industrial relations department about these typical time frames. For new hires, do not be surprised by time frames of 80 days for hourly employees and six months for salaried engineers.

Benefits Visibility

Does management communicate to employees their actual benefits? In most instances, employees are ignorant of what they are acutally paid by the company in terms of salary and benefits. Today in most medium-to-large companies, the employee benefits take-home-pay ratio is in the 35 to 50 percent range. Health and dental packages, FICA, pension, liberal vacations (two to five weeks), medical absences, etc., are not always well known by those benefiting from them. Employees should be aware of the total salary and benefits they actually earn.

Monthly or quarterly division bulletins highlighting these areas as well as communicating important events should be used. For the best results, they should be mailed to the employee's home. Annual reports to the stockholders should also be prepared detailing the important events of the preceding year, the key objectives for the future period, and explaining the major aspects of the hidden pay; e.g., the average medical and dental payback (the average medical and dental payback for the past year was $1,860 per employee, the average loss for inexcusable absenteeism was 6.7 days, etc.). Strategically located poster boards could also detail these same figures.

Safety Program

Does the company have a documented safety program to prevent mishaps that result in cost increase, project impact, or loss or damage to human life? It is very important that in today's heavily regulated environment companies have a comprehensive safety program. The program should start with training at new employee orientation, update training for supervisors, and brief top management periodically on injury rates, days lost to injuries, workmen's compensation rates, and OSHA recordable case filings. The employee suggestion program should make provisions for safety improvements in the work areas. A safety committee should be established with the task of doing periodic walk through audits. It is amazing how people from different departments can identify safety violations and suggest improvements outside their own areas.

Finance

Business today is moving quickly to keep up with the international arena. Techniques of finance and cost accounting have to be used with greater intelligence and sureness than ever before. A firm's financial management control system is actually a collection of integrated subsystems that provide a formal means by which top management runs a business. The accounting and finance departments are integral parts of many other functional areas; that is, information is generated by marketing, manufacturing, engineering, personnel, quality, and so on, which then becomes input for accounting and finance to issue timely management and operational reports. In turn, their meaningful reports serve as input for planning and controlling diverse organizational activities.

Responsibility and Authority

Does the company have documented procedures for identifying and describing responsibilities and authorities to be assigned to each functional area? Company and division directives, standard procedures, etc., are important parts of internal communications to document the methodology proven through time and use. Figure 21 shows a typical division functional overview. Depending on the size of the corporation and the division, the number and extent of the standard practices will vary. The impact of standard practices is shown in Figure 22 for part of the procurement and material functions at our $500 million sales division.

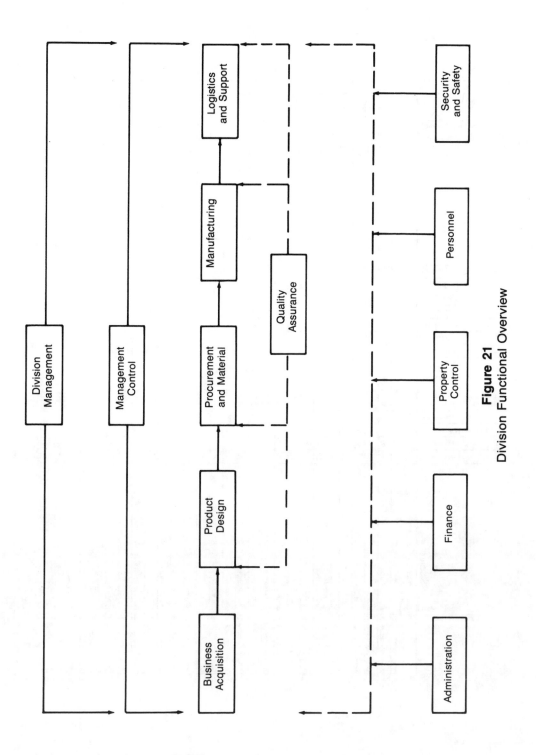

Figure 21
Division Functional Overview

Subject — Procurement and Material, Section 6	Customer/Air Force	GD Corporate Office	GD/FW Top Management	F-16 Program Office	Research and Engineering	Material	Finance	F-111 Program Office	Logistics and Support	Production	F-16 Production Management	Manufacturing	Tooling and MSE	Prod. Planning and Control	Manufacturing Development	Plant Services	Industrial Engineering	Marketing	Quality Assurance	Contracts and Estimating	Special Projects	F-16XL Program Office	F-16 Internat Prog. Office	General Counsel — Legal	Productivity	Industrial Relations	Public Affairs	Electronic Products	Data Systems Division
Procurement	X	X				X	X																	X					
Special Order Request	X	X	X			X	X			X																X			X
Advance Material Release		X	X		X	X	X									X			X										X
Technical, Consultant and Contract Personnel Services					X	X	X	X							X		X	X								X			
Receiving	X					X	X		X																				
Receiving — Over, Short or Damaged Shipments	X	X			X	X	X		X	X		X	X	X		X	X		X					X					X
Incoming Shipments Lost in Transit	X	X				X	X		X			X		X		X								X					X
Borrowing Material					X	X								X															
Loaning Material	X	X				X										X													
Premium Cost Transportation	X				X	X	X		X	X				X		X			X					X					
Outside Production Procurement Authorization		X	X	X		X		X		X	X	X	X	X								X	X						
Procurement of Outside Production Tasks					X	X				X	X	X	X	X						X		X	X						
Material Furnished or Sold to Suppliers	X	X			X	X	X	X		X	X	X	X	X		X			X	X		X	X						
Outside Production Task Transfer	X	X	X	X	X	X	X	X		X	X	X	X	X	X	X	X		X	X		X	X	X				X	
Experimental, Developmental or Research Procurements	X			X	X	X								X	X					X									
Returnable Containers	X	X				X					X	X		X					X										
Nitrogen Storage and Coversion			X		X	X		X	X	X		X		X		X			X			X	X			X			
Visits and Assignments to Supplier Plants	X	X	X		X	X	X	X								X	X		X			X	X			X		X	
Supplier Termination and Obsolescence Claims		X	X		X	X	X	X	X					X					X	X		X	X						
Supplier Contacts			X		X	X	X	X	X									X	X									X	
Qualification of Materials and Processes						X													X										
Petty Cash			X			X	X									X													
Special Supplier Selection	X	X	X		X	X		X					X			X			X			X	X			X		X	
Procurement Subcontract Management		X	X		X	X	X	X												X		X	X					X	

Figure 22

Standard Practices Impact on Specific Organizations

Indirect Costs Management

Does the company have an adequate system for managing and controlling indirect costs? Annual operating budgets and long-range plans are the key documents used by companies for financial control and cost planning. Well-defined policies and procedures are essential to ensure orderly collection of all pertinent data that must be considered when establishing these plans. Once operating budgets have been established and approved by top management, they become the benchmark for managing cost performance — some of these are covered in *Part Two, Key Management Information System Indicators* (page 11). Actual costs are compared with budgeted costs, and variance analysis is done monthly on significant locations, both positive and negative. Variance and reasons for these plus or minus deviations are elevated to management for corrective actions.

In the past three to five years of recession, the profitable surviving companies are now trying to be leaner and more productive. Most of the fat has been cut in the obvious places; warehouse inventories, work-in-process, factory labor, etc. But top management really has to poke into areas that middle managers fear to explore because they are much harder to identify. The following are the most likely places to find the last good cuts:

- Services are added with computers and automated office equipment with no cuts in people, reports, or paperwork.
- Minimum order levels, repricing procurements, and the actual costs to do some jobs should be analyzed. If you don't know what a lot of these indirect costs are, they will never be changed.
- Few executives really need private secretaries. Overnight mail delivery is a fad and rarely essential — what is the dollar figure for your division or department? Word processors can actually increase the time to produce letters because it's so easy to keep changing them prior to mailing.

Cash Flow

Does the company have adequate controls to optimize cash flow, both paying and collecting? In many businesses today, the vice president of finance does not know what's going on in the factory, and consequently, does not "voucher" fast enough or often enough to collect what's due the company. In my reviews of different companies and divisions, I found that several insufficient scenarios existed:

- The production department lumped the deliveries together for a two-week billing cycle, then shipped the documents to finance for billing to the customer. An on-site contracts or finance person should bill immediately when items were ready, especially on high-dollar deliverables.
- The production department planned all its deliveries for the end of the month when, not only are they the busiest trying to meet that month's goals, but the paying customer is also swamped with other customers and excessive paperwork.

- Cash flow time is not optimized. Several companies still use ordinary mail versus electronic mail, or at least expedited mail procedures. Figure 23 shows what can be achieved by working with your major customers and the banking system. The customers that work with the Air Force Systems Command now have electronic transmission capability with both the customer and the banks and can pay within two days. The old expedited system took seven to 10 days. Some systems take up to 21 days!

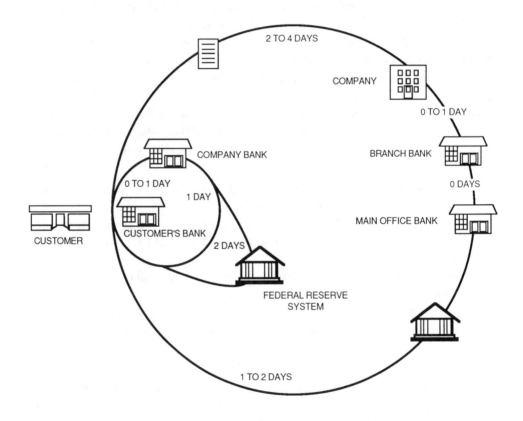

CIRCUMFERENCE	RANGE	AVERAGE
LARGE	3 TO 7 DAYS	5 DAYS
SMALL	1 TO 2 DAYS	2 DAYS

Figure 23
Cash Flow Time Comparison

Direct Costs Management

Does the company have an adequate system for tracking direct budgeted costs and schedule versus actual performance? Companies need some type of management control system to ensure that the contractor's management is systematically tracking cost and schedule. (In the government contracting arena, Department of Defense Instruction 7000.2, Cost/Schedule Control System Criteria defines the criteria for such a system.) The management control system should be detailed and objective enough to provide evidence concerning reasonableness of the estimate of completion, degree of baseline control, validity of work package adjustments, accuracy of variance analyses, effectiveness of corrective action, use of any management reserve, effects of contract changes on budgets and schedules, and subcontractor data. This system is used on large projects and usually handled by contractor program offices. The main thrust in this area is that the company should have only one basic system of books to track any size system. If you cannot adequately track and control the schedule and costs through the manufacturing and procurement departments, you will probably be out of control on costs — and that's what makes companies go bankrupt.

Cost Reduction and Value Control

Does the company have an effective cost reduction and value control program? The people that make up an organization are a manager's most valuable assets. To effectively use this resource, the basic philosophy of cost reduction should be carefully nurtured to reap this powerful, often hidden tool. The basic philosophy of the cost reduction and value control program should be:

A better job can be done. Every employee can do a better job in contributing to the value of our product. If we don't have the best design, the best material, the best methods, the best vendor, we can and must do a better job. Now, by the best we don't mean the most complicated, therefore the most costly; but the simplest way consistent with reliability that will perform the function.[27]

A thorough cost reduction program should provide the opportunity for all departments and personnel to reduce costs continually while maintaining or improving overall effectiveness. Some major areas to be considered for a comprehensive and proven program through recognition by the DOD and the Military Service Departments are:

- Value Control — Cost-reduction achievements normally associated with hardware-oriented savings such as changes in design, specifications, procurement, and manufacturing methods.
- Procurement Cost Improvement — Cost reduction achievements resulting from quantity buying, combining orders, establishing alternate sources, price analysis, negotiated price reductions with or without a related change in task or requirements, material substitutions, multiple use of assets, and use of surplus material.

- Resources Economics/Conversion — Cost reductions achieved through the installation and operation of more efficient capital-type industrial equipment. Cost reductions achieved in controllable overhead expenses such as utilities, stationery supplies, operating supplies, telephone, telegraph, travel, plumbing equipment, and lumber.
- Employee Suggestions — A formal program for employees to submit ideas to reduce costs and receive monetary awards for acceptable ideas.
- Productivity Improvement — Reduction in labor costs achieved through the application of worker measurement techniques, methods improvements, crew loading procedures, task control, and production improvements.
- Management Improvement — Cost reductions achieved in administrative areas or overhead functions through actions such as consolidation or combining of functions, improved organizational alignments, use of mechanical systems in place of manual procedures, improved operating procedures, and worker measurement.[28]

Engineering

Design engineering happens to be an area often overlooked in many companies today in the ongoing quest for quality products. Design is the starting point for effective cost, schedule, and quality product output. The customers want what they pay for — high quality, reliable products. Customers usually buy whatever they percieve as the best value product with little loyalty to any company, especially if they had trouble with a previous product purchased from that particular company. *Customers will forgive almost anything except poor quality and reliability!*

Objectives and Policies

Does the company have documented engineering objectives and policies that clearly define the engineering management system, and are they approved by the chief operating official? An engineering management system should cover the applicable hardware and embedded computer resource aspects of all elements which are generally related to managing engineering resources, design, system safety, reliability, maintainability, value engineering, configuration, and test. It is essential that delegation of authority and responsibility for all engineering requirements are assigned to specific elements of the company organization and that the delegations are in consonance with the stated engineering objectives of the company. The managerial system provides for periodic audits by properly designated company organizations to ensure continuing effectiveness of the engineering management system. This management system should have objectives or indicators that are, in effect, the sensors that measure progress, indicate current position relative to planned position, and alert the experienced manager to take timely corrective action. There are several ways to measure the "goodness" of the design, but the elements shown in Figure 24 are those highlighted by the Defense Science Board for both engineering and manufacturing.[29]

Design Trouble Indicators	Manufacturing Trouble Indicators
Schedule variance/milestone slippage	Schedule variance/milestone slippage
Cost variance	Cost variance
Design review findings	Work force turnover/attrition
Late CDRL items	Alternate methods of fabrication
Supplier/subcontractor performance	Parts shortages
Broken technical performance measurement threshold	Scrap rates
	Rework rates
Failure to maintain TAAF slope	Yield rate of screens
ECP rate	Test equipment lateness
Haywires per unit	Assembly nonconformances
Corrective-action activity	Assembly man-hour deviations from learning curve
Items in failure analysis	Bench-test time/anomalies
Change traffic	EIDP variability
	Items in failure analysis
	Corrective-action activity

Figure 24
Trouble Indicators

Design Management

Does the company have an adequate design management system? (Some appropriate references for military contractors are: MIL-STD-499A, MIL-STD-490, AFSCP 800-19, AFR 800-14, MIL-STD-891, MIL-Q-9858A, and MIL-STD-52779). Managers of the engineering and technical effort must transform a military requirement systematically into a coordinated and approved description of the hardware and/or software item produced. Contractors must conduct hardware and computer software internal design reviews not only to ensure that all design parameters are met, but also to ensure producibility and ease of inspection. Specialty engineering efforts including computer-aided design and parts control must be integrated into mainstream design results. Engineering decisions and trade-offs are necessary. The procedure governing this process must be adequate to ensure timely satisfaction of program needs.

Essential to a broad-based, effective design system are the "tools" for use by the designer(s). These, as a minimum, should include: (1) computer-aided design (CAD) terminals, along with computer-aided manufacturing (CAM); (2) standard parts, standard circuits, and duration criteria manual, and (3) closed-loop feedback system of manufacturing floor anomalies and data system for past, similar part designs. The CAD/CAM systems are tremendous innovations and documented improvements in quality and productivity can be increased dramatically. Where CAD is linked With CAM, reductions in labor of 30 to 1 and reductions in lead time of 50 to 1 are obtainable.[30]

Reliability Management

Does the company have an adequate reliability management system? (See MIL-STD-785.) An adequate management system for reliability must provide for both achievement and assurance, and it must be applied from early planning stages through design, development, production, and product improvement stages. Reliability assurance includes activities directed toward establishing appropriate reliability development goals, monitoring program activities, and evaluating results to verify that established goals are met. Reliability is a quantitative characteristic predictable in design, measurable in test, assurable in production, and maintainable in the field. Reliability is controllable and should be monitored and guided at each step of system development to ensure a high probability of program success.

Maintainability Program

Does the contractor have an adequate maintainability management system? (See MIL-STD-470.) An adequate management system for maintainability ensures that the design and development effort considers how the hardware can be maintained in minimum time, at low cost, and with a minimum expenditure of support resources (personnel, spare parts, tools and test equipment, services and support facilities), without adversely affecting performance or safety characteristics.

Value Engineering Management System

Does the company have an active, traceable value engineering (VE) management system? Value control was born through the necessity to drive costs down. It is a technique that supplements conventional cost reduction programs. Value control is a company-wide program of continuous and intensive appraisal of all elements influencing the cost of products and practices, and the elimination of those factors which adds to an item's cost, but which are not necessary for the required reliable functional performance. Value control includes VE, value analysis, value assurance, and value improvement. More simply defined, value control is an organized approach to determine the function of a part, procedure, or process, to place a price tag on the function, and to find a way to provide the function at the lowest total cost.

Knowing more about value should cause the term value control to take on new meaning. Here is the basic philosophy that makes up the value control approach:

> A better job can be done. Every employee can do a better job in contributing to the value of our product. If we don't have the best design, the best material, the best methods, and the best vendor, we can and must do a better job. By the best we don't mean the most complicated, therefore the most costly, but the simplest, most reliable way that will perform the function. Value control requires a team effort of all persons involved with product design, production, and procurement pulling together to accomplish the best results.

Both the VE Incentive Clause and the VE Program Requirement Clause of government contracts encourage value engineering change proposals. This includes proposals that would produce collateral savings in government-furnished property, operations, maintenance, embedded computer resources, or other areas, and that do not impair any essential function or characteristic. VE Incentive Clauses provide for the contractor to share in any real savings which accrue to the government resulting from contractor-initiated proposals. To be acceptable the proposal must also involve some change in the contract specifications, purchase description, or statement of work. The VE Incentive Clause encourages the contractor to engage in value engineering. In contrast, the VE Program Requirement Clause obligates the contractor to engage in value engineering to the level and scope required by an item or work in the contract schedule. The principal reason for requiring a VE program is to ensure early results in the initial stages of a system life cycle where changes are fairly easy to accomplish and savings may be large. An adequate program requires VE objectives, policies, procedures, responsibilities, and reporting requirements to be formally established. It is vitally important that the contractor's top management periodically review the VE program to ensure implementation and continuing attention by middle management.

Test Management System

Does the contractor have an adequate test management system? (See MIL-Q-9858A, AFR 800-3, AFR 80-14, and MIL-S-52779.) An adequate test management system must provide overall guidance of how hardware and computer software tests will be managed. This guidance is aimed at managers above the program manager level. The contractor's policies and procedures address the management of development, qualification, and acceptance tests relative to configuration items and their system(s). The policies and procedures also address computer hardware and software management tests relative to planning, organization, coordination, knowledge of current status, and control of documentation.

Contractor test management policy should be comprised of five major elements generically ingrained in the organizational structure and specifically integrated for each program under contract. These five elements are: (1) program management, (2) test program manager (assigned to program office), (3) design/systems engineering, (4) testing organization, and (5) test monitoring organization (reliability and/or quality assurance).

The test monitoring organization must be organizationally independent of the program office and design/systems engineering to assure complete organizational freedom in ascertaining compliance to test plans, proper failure analyses, timely corrective action, required retesting, and reporting to contractor top management.

The contractor's internal procedures must clearly set forth test management policy, organizational responsibilities, and the need for plans and procedures, and provide the basis for adequate test facility acquisition. Detailed policy and guidance must be provided regarding testing concepts and objectives, the development and ultimate use of technical data, the translation of test requirements into test plans and procedures, and how all these areas are funded, managed, and coordinated with the customer.

The contractor's program manager is responsible for establishing program test requirements with the customer and assuring that contract documentation accurately reflects the critical issues to be resolved by test and evaluation. This documentation should also provide a summary of test objectives, schedules, resources, funding obligations, milestones, and reporting requirements. This also includes the establishment of a tracking system for deficiencies and effective, timely resolution of these deficiencies.

The test and evaluation requirements should not only be tailored for a specific program, but must also be tailored to each phase of the program. Test and evaluation is required as a minimum for the following kinds of systems:

- New or existing systems.
- One-of-a-kind system.
- Commercial off-the-shelf item.
- Modification program.
- Computer system, subsystem, or component.

Test and evaluation is tailored for these typical program phases:

- Design concept exploration.
- Design and development.
- Full-scale development.
- Production and deployment.

Test concepts and objectives must be developed for design and development, qualification, reliability, production acceptance, and operational test and evaluation which address the critical issues and also provide for integration of maintainability demonstrations and tests. All of these items must be integrated in matrix fashion into a test and evaluation master plan. The master plan must be prepared during the conceptual design phase and reviewed and updated at the start of each subsequent phase of the program.

Design concepts must take into account testability characteristics which would simplify testing and aid fault isolation. Consideration for use of self-test and built-in-test equipment must be included in the design trade studies as well as how much of the testing is to be automatic versus manual. Test and evaluation may be done to help select the preferred alternative concepts during the design concept exploration phase.

During the design and development phase, test and evaluation is conducted to minimize design risks and demonstrate feasibility of the breadboard item of working to a desired level. It also helps in making the trade-offs that will best satisfy operational requirements. Subsystems, components, system prototypes, or preproduction articles are tested to develop data for making a full-scale engineering development decision. While this testing is primarily development test and evaluation, the customer may also require (or elect to perform) operational test and evaluation at this time to look at the operational aspects of the testing approach. During this phase, long lead items for test and evaluation should be identified and procurement actions initiated. Also, systems should be evaluated in a realistic, multiple use environment to identify potential vulnerabilities that should be corrected before or during the next acquisition phase.

During the full-scale development phase, development test and evaluation is done to make sure that the engineering is reasonably complete and that the most important design problems have been identified and solved. Initial operational tests and evaluations are usually conducted during this phase using a prototype, preproduction article, or a pilot production item as the test vehicle in performance-oriented tests, to estimate the operational effectiveness and suitability of the system.

During the production and deployment phase, development test and evaluation is conducted to evaluate product improvements and changes to reduce system life cycle costs and increase reliability, maintainability, and availability. Operational test and evaluation is conducted to refine estimates of operational effectiveness and suitability, to examine any modifications or changes, and to see whether the system meets operational needs in changing environments. Qualification tests, and reliability and maintainability demonstration tests are conducted early in the production phase. Production acceptance tests are conducted early in the production phase. Production acceptance tests are conducted on each delivered article to assure compliance with requirements.

Quantitative performance objectives and evaluation criteria are established for computer software during each system acquisition phase. Testing should be structured to demonstrate that software has reached a level of maturity appropriate to each phase. Such performance objectives and evaluation criteria are established for both full-system and casualty mode operations. For embedded software, performance objectives and evaluation criteria are included in the performance objectives and evaluation criteria of the overall system. Before release for operational use, software developed for either new or existing systems should undergo sufficient operational testing as part of the total system to provide a valid estimate of system effectiveness and suitability in the operational environment. Such testing includes combined hardware, software, and interface testing under realistic conditions, using typical operator personnel. The evaluation of test results includes an assessment of operational performance under other possible conditions that were not used, but which could occur during operational use.

Tests conducted during all program acquisition phases must be planned, funded, and conducted according to customer-approved test plans, procedures, facilities, test equipment, and test articles. This includes testing conducted to assess the operational impact of candidate technical approaches and to determine preferred alternative concepts (that is, operational demonstrations, feasibility tests, requirements definitions, conceptual demonstrations, etc.).

Contractor program managers must integrate a reliability and maintainability (R&M) readiness, sustainability, and logistic supportability test and evaluation effort into the overall test and evaluation program. Specifically, field activity should be implemented to make sure adequate data is collected, R&M and logistic support factors (such as the maintenance concept, handbooks, support equipment, spares, and training) are assessed and R&M deficiencies are identified. The test effort will focus on user concerns and issues, such as inservice use suitability and supportability, and user-oriented testing. It will help determine if the systems and support subsystems can be operated and maintained by user personnel under conditions projected for use.

Figure 25 illustrates the major steps from design concept through volume production for a typical component, subsystem, or system. The chart is simplified to show the important role that data analysis, problem resolution, and corrective action have in developing a mature, reliable product. A well-planned and executed test and evaluation program has important beneficial effects for the contractor. Some of these benefits are:

- Engineering changes are minimized and concentrated at the start of the program.
- Potential problems in the design and manufacturing process are readily identified and avoided by advance planning.
- Reliability is benchmarked and controlled from the start, eliminating the need for hurried reliability improvement programs.
- Production costs, warranty costs, and service contracts for the product rapidly become stable and valid, allowing realistic planning and allocations.
- Customers receive reliable products that perform as expected.
- A well-controlled, reliable configuration simplifies training, field service, and spare-part logistics.

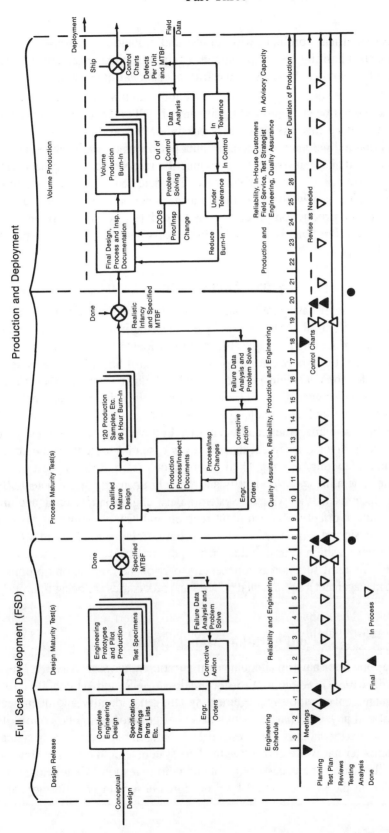

Figure 25

Design Release Through Controlled Volume Production

The most significant problem with all test and evaluation programs consists of three elements: (1) simulated environments, (2) limited number of items for test, and (3) a limited number of items in the true operational environment.

Since this is true, commitments for production quantities are attended by an unknown risk that has been minimized significantly by all of the testing done before production. To reduce this risk as soon as possible after production has started, it is essential that a timely and accurate product performance feedback system be in place in the field and that contractor personnel be responsive for implementing effective corrective action to prevent recurrence. The field data are especially important since the product is now operating in its true use environment and the products in use represent the production process. This field data, used properly and in a timely fashion, can significantly reduce life cycle costs with an attendant improvement in reliability.

Safety Engineering

Does the contractor have an adequate system safety engineering management system? (See MIL-STD-882.) System saftey engineering involves the application of scientific and engineering principles for the timely identification of hazards and initiation of those actions necessary to prevent or control hazards in the system. It draws on professional knowledge and specialized skills in the mathematical, physical, and related science disciplines, together with the principles and methods of engineering design and analysis to specify, predict, and evaluate the safety of the system. Effective management and integration of the efforts of the professional personnel in these diverse technical disciplines is essential to achieve the stated goals of system safety engineering. Their efforts should start at the earliest possible time in the system life cycle to identify and then eliminate or control potentially unacceptable hazards to the system. System safety engineering techniques are required to result in effective hazard identification and risk assessment. Also, if nuclear safety design requirements exist, the program plan should address them in a comprehensive fashion to ensure that the proper criteria are effectively applied to the system. An audit function is a necessary part of the contractor's program to ensure that management's documented policies and procedures are being rigorously followed.

Configuration Management

Does the contractor have an adequate configuration management system? (See MIL-STD-490, MIL-STD-483, MIL-S-480, MIL-S-52779, and AFR 800-14 vol. II.) An adequate configuration management system must identify and document the functional and physical characteristics of a configuration item and control its changes. The contractor should have an established configuration management system relative to computer hardware and software. This system should describe how the contractor will perform the necessary tasks and who is responsible for doing the work. Included in the system should be procedures describing the development of configuration identification, the control of engineering changes, and accounting for the status of the documentation and associated hardware and software.

The configuration of an item is its functional and physical characteristics as described in technical documents and achieved in the end item. Examples of functional characteristics are range, speed, reliability, availability, etc. Physical characteristics include descriptions such as composition, dimensions, form, fit, finishes, etc.

Configuration management is the engineering discipline of identifying, controlling, accounting, and auditing the functional and physical characteristics of items. The primary purpose of these four functions is to ensure operational efficiency and control cost. Configuration identification is the discipline of selecting the documents that identify and define the configuration characteristics of an item. These documents usually refer to specifications and drawings for hardware, but may include flow charts or decision trees for software. Configuration control is the process of controlling changes to the configuration and its identification documents. Configuration status accounting is the process of recording and reporting the implementation of changes to the configuration and its identification documents. Configuration auditing is the process of checking and verifying that an item is in compliance with its configuration identification. There are two types of audits during the acquisition process. A functional configuration audit is performed to verify if the functional performance of an item meets its specification requirements. A physical configuration audit is performed to verify that the "as built" version of an item matches the approved and released documentation that describes the item.

Understanding the basic concepts of configuration management is the first step in examining configuration control on a more detailed basis. Engineering changes are limited to those necessary and beneficial to the customer. Managers must ensure all recommended engineering changes meet one of the following four criteria: (1) deficiency correction, (2) change in user requirements, (3) substantial life-cycle cost savings, or (4) prevention or permission for desired slippage in an approved schedule. Configuration control provides a program manager the means by which proposed engineering changes can receive the necessary management scrutiny and prioritization.

Effective management of engineering changes requires an orderly process of recommended changes through the following six steps: (1) justify the need, (2) establish the change as Class I or Class II, (3) prepare an engineering change proposal, (4) submit to and review by the customer (5) approve or disapprove classification, and (6) incorporate the change in the item and data. Managers who recognize the importance and need for each of these steps are well on their way to successful configuration control.

The most important aspect of configuration control is tracking your product when it gets in the hands of the customer. If a problem arises, then knowing the status and whereabouts of your product is the ultimate when recalls, warranties, and fixability implementation are necessary.

Engineering Quality Improvement

Does the company have an engineering quality improvement training program? In 1982, recognizing that increased management emphasis on quality has produced notable results in many products (especially in those from Japan) and responding to the challenge of the U.S. military services to reduce the "15 percent hidden costs" in factory scrap and rework, General Dynamics launched a quality improvement program. Its three principal ingredients are: (1) management involvement, (2) quality measurement with annually tightened goals, and (3) extensive training. In 1983, the engineering department of the Pomona division created a training program to change the attitudes of 1,300 engineers and provide them with tools and principles for improving the quality of their work and products.[31] The objectives were:

- Understand the elements of in-use, in-house quality.
- Raise the level of priority on quality.
- Improve the principles and tools for achieving quality.

Because of the QIP dictum for management involvement, division managers were used as instructors rather than outside experts. The costs would be lower, the instruction would be more convincing, and managers would simultaneously learn by teaching. But while the supervisors were experienced in giving lecture presentations, they were not well versed in the kind of listening and adapting that is required when leading a seminar. So instruction in seminar techniques as well as in methods of improving quality had to be given to the instructors. Also, since this training activity would be a substantial increase in their already busy work load, the training schedule had to be spread out to allow for course planning as well as the actual leading of seminars. The structuring of the classes and designation of instructors was assigned to organization management. The QIP training basics are listed as follows:

- Every engineer is trained.
- Classes are interactive seminars.
- Seminars are led by the boss.
- All levels of management have responsibilities.
- Off-site instructors' courses are concentrated on fundamentals such as designing for quality, reliability, supportability, and techniques in conducting a seminar.
- In-plant engineers' seminars are tailored to fit functions.

To create the syllabus and present the topics, the division organized a committee of managers from the systems engineering, design, test, and logistics disciplines. The reliability manager acted as chairman. Training specialists were brought in to teach and demonstrate seminar leadership techniques. A top executive was scheduled to speak each day. Customers and users were brought in to express their views of the need for better quality in our products.

The course outline and all of the presentations were reviewed by the top managers of the departments. The presentations were rehearsed, videotaped, and critiqued by the course committee. At off-site courses, the presentations and discussion periods were videotaped for later use by the seminar instructors. Hard copies of all the presentation material were distributed in a special notebook. The topics covered in the course are listed in Figure 26.

• Keynote Address	• Designing for Testability
• Understanding the Development Process	• Designing for Reliable Software
• Designing to Requirements	• Understanding the Factory
• Designing for Simplicity and Balance	• Designing for Producibility
• Understanding Reliability	• User's View
• Reliability versus Complexity	• Designing for the User
• Disciplines for Reliable Design	• Program Office View
• Environments and Screens	• Instruction Methods
• Test Operations View	• Course Tailoring Guidelines

Figure 26
Instructor's Syllabus

The length of the training course for each of the engineers was 20 hours. It was found in prior technical training courses that it is possible to teach a new technical subject in this length of time, but more importantly, this figure represented an acceptable financial expenditure within the overhead budget that was established. The guidelines suggested that the course be conducted in 10 classes of two hours each, but some instructors found it more convenient to hold 20 one-hour sessions.

The payoff for General Dynamics has been impressive. The corporation is implementing the training at its other divisions and many measurements have been developed to allow engineers and management to measure the quality of the design output.

Program Management

One of the most important ideas of modern times has been the systems approach: the solution of a complete problem in its environment by an orderly process of assembling the parts required to solve the whole problem. The systems approach makes it possible to solve problems that were once considered too complicated. In essence, the systems approach starts by defining the goals and is followed by the blend of people, materials, and equipment that will solve the problem. It includes the building of the solution and results in the implementation of the solution.

The systems approach exists today because of the technological advances and scientific breakthroughs that have accompanied the enormous growth of business and government. The more complex the problem, the more necessary it becomes to use the systems approach. In the future, business and government will be even more influenced by the need for advances in complex problem areas. It is this combination of need and complexity that makes a situation subject to the systems approach.

Implementation of the system approach requires project management. A project has a single set of objectives; achieving them represents completion of the project. These objectives often involve research, development, design, manufacture, and construction or installation of hardware, but they may also include completion of a study, development of computer software, or similar activities not involving hardware. Activities centering on hardware may be treated as a separate project for a while and then included in the normal stream of business; for example, the market research, design, initial production, and initial market launching of a product may be treated as a project, after which the project organization is disbanded and the product is managed as a part of normal activity. A project has a finite and well-defined life span. It is not an activity that will continue as a normal part of the organization's existence. It is good to keep in mind that although project management disciplines and practices are part of managing any continuing organization, all individual projects come to an end. They may be replaced, but always by projects that are equally distinct. Many projects have exceeded their useful life at unnecessary cost because, at the outset of the project, general management did not ask the highly relevant question, "How can we tell when it's finished?"[32]

The most important feature of any reasonable program management approach is the appointment of the project manager. The manager running a project must be a zealot for the project and have full authority and responsibility to direct the company's activities on the project.

Documented System

Does the contractor have a documented project management system? A project management system should cover all elements that are generally related to the management of proposals, contract administration, budgeting, cost or schedule control, subcontract management, auditing, and reporting. The contractor identifies the organization(s) responsible for these functions. It is essential that the delegation of authority and responsibility for all project management tasks are assigned to specific elements of the contractor's organization and in consonance with the stated project management objectives of the company. The management system provides for periodic internal audits to ensure continuing management effectiveness.

Training Program

Does the company have a development training program for program manager? Although experience in a functional organization is a good start, a good program manager needs a lot of skills to go along with a dynamic managerial style. This can be provided in-house if the company or organization is large enough, but it can also be obtained at select universities or, for government contractors, Defense System Management School, Fort Blevoir, Virginia. Figure 27 lists the program phases for a DOD project, the internal and external program influences, and a suggested phase training agenda.

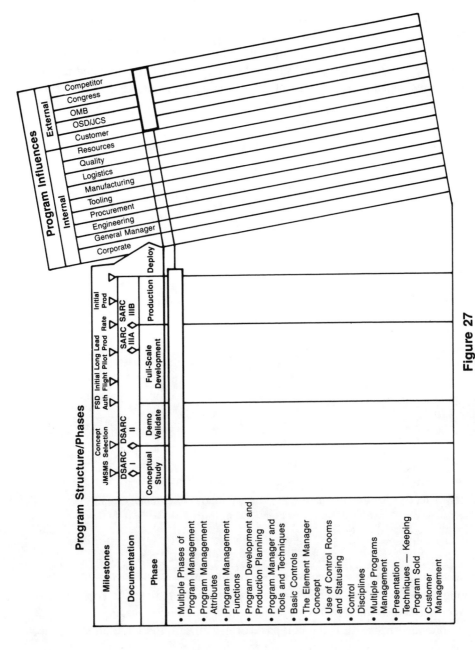

Figure 27

Program Manager Requirements/Interfaces

Once the program manager has been selected, trained, and started on the project, he or she should keep an important document handy as a ready reference. This document is DOD Directive 4245.7 "Transition from Development to Production".[33] This document is a series of templates that emphasizes the assurance of design, measurement of test stability, and certification of the manufacturing process. These templates are used to facilitate "discipline" in the total program process. This document was created by a Defense Service Board Task Force and it is still adding to the templates. The document face cover and template categories are shown in Figures 28 and 29.

Solving the Risk Equation in Transitioning from Development to Production

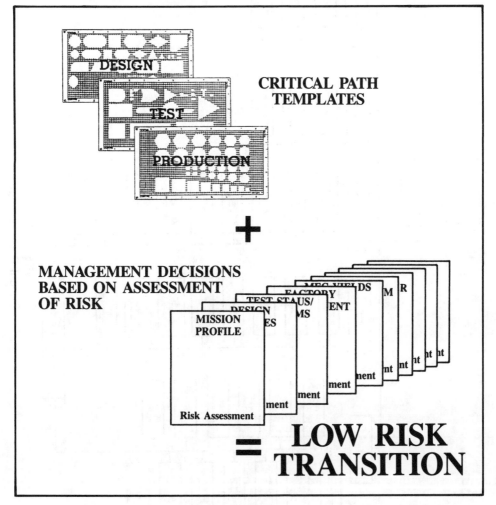

Figure 28
Solving the Risk Equation in Transitioning
from Development to Production

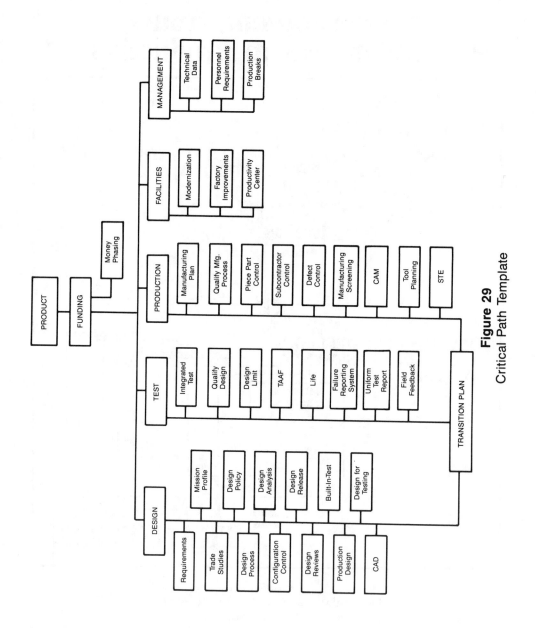

Figure 29
Critical Path Template

Customer Supremacy

Does the program manager know, have a listing of, and visit schedule for the customer? One of the most important tenets of program management is to know thy customer. The customer is supreme. It is most important for the program manager to know who the customers are during each phase of the program, as noted in Figure 30 (example of the U.S. Army Readiness Command).

Department of Army Readiness Command

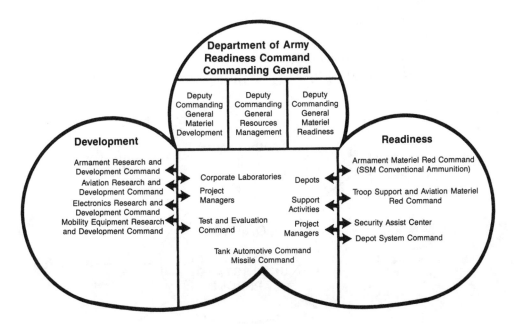

Figure 30
Customer Organization Chart

Management Information System

Does the program manager have a MIS to report significant problems, cost, schedule, quality, or technical status to appropriate management levels? The program manager has to be involved in many areas to control the total program (Figure 31). If involvement is given up on any of these elements, the program manager is no longer in control of the total program. These elements are more fully illustrated in Figure 32 for the major phases of the program. This breakdown should then cover selected phases such as production. Production program management tools are developed at General Dynamics' divisions to provide enough visibility to control the following:

- Factory costs by department or function.
- Support costs by department or function.
- Are purchase orders being placed?
- Purchased part shortages.
- Daily and weekly schedule.
- Spare part delivery status.
- Drawing and ECP status.
- Tool design and fabrication status.
- Test equipment design and manufacturing status.
- Test procedure development status.
- Test yields.
- Process yields.
- Scrap and rework.
- Quality and reliability.
- Program action items.

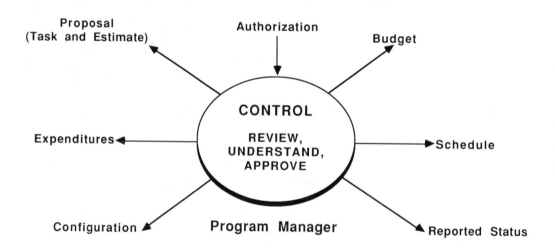

Figure 31
Program Manager Control

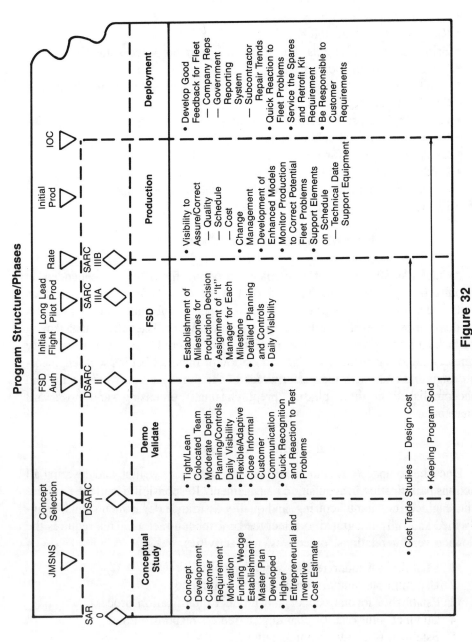

Figure 32

Program Manager Requirements/Interface

Is the program manager really using innovative methods? Most excellent managers really know how to lead using a variety of "tricks of the trade":

- Keep program team "lean and mean."
- Rotate the best through the program office.
- Give urgent work to busy people.
- Know when to "kill the engineer."
- Bring me your problems, but also bring your proposed solutions.
- If it's not broken, don't fix it.
- Good news I like to receive; bad news I must receive, but it must be timely.
- Show confidence in your people.
- Give people a pat on the back.
- Recognize personal achievements.
- Extra point award for performance appraisals.
- Chide slip-ups.
- Shoot yourself in the foot award for mistakes or goof-ups.
- Keep an open door and lend an open ear.

Procurement and Subcontracts

As much as 50 percent of a company's program funds may be expended on subcontracts and complex purchase orders. The success of a firm depends as much on effective source selection, pricing, and management of subcontractors and vendors as it does on the control of in-house manufactured work. Executive management must have an acute appreciation of the importance of material in achieving satisfactory prime contractor performance. The acquisition of material begins with engineering design and ends with the performance of the purchased part or system, and is accomplished in three phases: prepurchasing, purchasing, and postaward management.

Functional Participation

Does the company have current procurement policies written and covering all functions participating in acquisition management? Responsibilities in the procurement, engineering, manufacturing, and quality assurance departments must be intertwined and fully integrated to select the best subcontractors. This requires the following vendor relations, objectives, and activities:

1. Establish a vendor relations quality policy.
2. Use multiple vendors for major procurements.
3. Establish a formal vendor and product qualification process.
4. Conduct joint quality planning; agree on responsibilities.
5. Establish two-way communication.
6. Set up to detect and remedy deviations.
7. Conduct vendor surveillance.
8. Exchange inspection data; provide certification.

9. Undertake improvement programs; set up mutual assistance.
10. Create and use vendor quality ratings.[34]

Of these activities, numbers 3, 5, 6, and 10 are required in most purchase situations. The need for the remaining activities depends on what is being bought. Modern products bought in large volume require the entire list of these activities. Traditional products, materials, and standard components use numbers 2 and 8. Proprietary products, produced to vendor specifications, are often bought by customers who lack test facilities and who therefore rely on vendors plus feedback from their own use. Where the pattern of products and purchases is a mixture, the buyers face the added problem of assuring that purchase of modern products is done with modern methods while purchase of traditional products continues to be done mainly with traditional methods.

Precontractual Actions

Does the company have a documented system for determining and controlling precontractual actions? A company should have an adequate system of checks and balances for the procurement personnel to follow. One of the best systems the author has encountered to date is the record documentation used by the U.S. Air Force Contract Management Division, Kirtland AFB, New Mexico. The forms used in this system are shown on pages 82-85. The record system may be too grandiose for those not involved in government contracts, but it is a fertile launching ground for any tailored procurement system.

PURCHASE ORDER/SUBCONTRACT/IDWA REVIEW RECORD

REVIEWER(S) (Organization/Initials) _____ DATE _____

☐ UNDER $10K ☐ $10K TO $25K ☐ $25K TO $100K ☐ $100K TO $500K ☐ $500K AND OVER ☐ IDWA ☐ CONSENT REVIEW

	CUSTOMER		PURCHASE ORDER OR SUBCONTRACT IDENTIFICATION				DISCOUNT TERMS	CHANGES ISSUED		ORDER TYPE	TYPE ORDER JUSTIFIED (Y or N)	LOW DOLLAR ORDER (Y or N)	IDWA ISSUE AND CONTROL	IDWA TARGET COST NEGOTIATED	COST ACCT STANDARDS DAR 3-1200 FAR PART 30		LINE NUMBER
LINE NUMBER	CONTRACT NUMBER	CONTRACT TYPE	DMS RATING (Y or N)	PURCHASE ORDER NUMBER	NAME OF VENDOR	ITEM DESCRIPTION	VALUE OF ORIGINAL ORDER		NUMBER	NET DOLLAR(S) CHANGE						APPLI-CABLE (Y or N)	OBTAINED (Y or N)	
	1	2	3	4	5	6	7	8	9	10	11	12	13	14	15	16	17	
1																		1
2																		2
3																		3
4																		4
5																		5
6																		6
7																		7
8																		8
9																		9
10																		10
11																		11
12																		12
13																		13
14																		14
15																		15

CODES: A - Adequate; D - Deficient; NA - Not Applicable

NOTE: If a column does not apply to the dollar category, draw a line down through it.

AFSC FORM 906 JUL 85   REPLACES AFCMD FORM 6, MAR 84, WHICH IS OBSOLETE   PAGE 1 OF 4 PAGES

LINE NUMBER	SPARES ORDERS					DETERMINATION OF REQUIREMENTS - LEAD TIME										SOURCE SELECTION AND COMPETITION						LINE NUMBER
						REQUISITION				DELIVERY						NUMBER OF BIDS						
	SPARES ONLY (*Y or N*)	COMPARED TO PRIOR YEAR PRICES (*Y or N*)	SPLIT AWARD (*Y or N*)	ITEM SUBJECT TO COMPONENT BREAKOUT (*Y or N*)	VENDOR RATING SYSTEM CHECKED (*Y or N*)	ORIGINAL DATE	DATE RECEIVED IN PURCHASING	MATERIAL REQUIRED DATE	PURCHASE ORDER DATE	LEAD TIME PROVIDED (*Days*) *24 vs 25*	PROMISED DATE	NO. OF CALENDAR DAYS SHORT *25 vs 28*	ACTUAL DELIVERY DATE	NO. OF DAYS DELINQUENT *28 vs 30*	DEFINITIZED IN 180 DAYS/ 40% PRODUCTION OF SUPPLIES/ PERFORMANCE OF WORK (*Y or N*)	REQUESTED	RECEIVED	RESPONSIVE	AWARD PRICE COMPETITIVE (*Y or N*)	PRICE COMPETITION TRIED BUT INEFFECTIVE BECAUSE	IF AWARD TO OTHER THAN LOW BIDDER, STATE REASON	
	18	19	20	21	22	23	24	25	26	27	28	29	30	31	32	33	34	35	36	37	38	
1																						1
2																						2
3																						3
4																						4
5																						5
6																						6
7																						7
8																						8
9																						9
10																						10
11																						11
12																						12
13																						13
14																						14
15																						15

AFSC FORM JUL 85 **906** REPLACES AFCMD FORM 6, MAR 84, WHICH IS OBSOLETE

PAGE 2 OF 4 PAGES

LINE NUMBER	39 SOLE OR SINGLE SOURCE (S or SS)	40 PRINCIPAL REASON CODE (A,B,C,D,E,F,G)[1]	41 ACCEPTABLE (Y or N)	42 PRE-AWARD SURVEY	43 TECH REVIEW PRE-AWARD	44 PRICE ANALYSIS APPLICABLE (Y or N)	45 ACCOMPLISHED (Y or N)	46 DONE EFFECTIVELY (Y or N)	47 PARTIAL OR FULL COST ANALYSIS[2] APPLICABLE (Y or N)	48 ACCOMPLISHED (Y or N)	49 DONE EFFECTIVELY (Y or N)	50 COST OR PRICING DATA (DD 633/SF 1411 or equal) APPLICABLE (Y or N)	51 OBTAINED (Y or N)	52 PRICE CERTIFICATE APPLICABLE (Y or N)	53 OBTAINED (Y or N)	54 AUDIT/PRICE ASSIST CONTRACTOR (Y, N, NA)	55 GOVERNMENT (Y, N, NA)	56 RATE VERIFICATION (Y or N)	57 OTHER (Y or N)	58 TECHNICAL ANALYSIS[2] APPLICABLE (Y or N)	59 DONE EFFECTIVELY (Y or N)	60 NEGOTIATION[2] APPLICABLE (Y or N)	61 CONDUCTED (Y or N)	62 DONE EFFECTIVELY (Y or N)	63 DEFECTIVE COST/PRICING DATA/AUDIT CLAUSES APPLICABLE (Y or N)	64 INCLUDED (Y or N)	65 PROGRESS PAYMENTS (Y or N)	66 FLOWDOWN T & C SPECIFICATIONS/STANDARDS	67 SMALL BUSINESS PLAN ($500K+) DAR 7-104.14(b) FAR 52.219-9	68 LABOR SURPLUS ($500K+) DAR 7-104.20 FAR 52.220-4	LINE NUMBER
1																															1
2																															2
3																															3
4																															4
5																															5
6																															6
7																															7
8																															8
9																															9
10																															10
11																															11
12																															12
13																															13
14																															14
15																															15

[1] A - Customer Directed; B - Engineering Directed; C - Proprietary Item; D - Only Supplier Qualified; E - Economically Justified; F - Other Justifiable Reason; G - Inadequate or No Justification.

[2] Required when Cost or Pricing Data/Certificates not required but Price Analysis alone does not verify Fair and Reasonable Price.

AFSC FORM 906 JUL 85 — REPLACES AFCMD FORM 6, MAR 84, WHICH IS OBSOLETE

LINE NUMBER	EEO CLAUSES, CERTIFICATIONS, REPRESENTATIONS									ACO						FOR OPTIONAL USE							REMARKS (Include AFCMD Form 97, Reference Number)	LINE NUMBER
										ADVANCE NOTIFICATION		WRITTEN JUSTIFICATION		PRIOR CONSENT										
	EEO CLAUSE ($10K+) DAR 7-103.18/ FAR 52.222-26	PRE-AWARD EEO CLEARANCE ($1M+) DAR 7-104.22/FAR 52.222-28	CERTIFICATE OF NONSEGREGATED FACILITIES ($10K+) DAR 7-2003.14(b) (1) (A) FAR 52.222-21	PREVIOUS CONTRACTS AND COMPLIANCE REPORTS ($10K+) DAR 7-2003.14(b) (1) (B) FAR 52.222-22	AFFIRMATIVE ACTION COMPLIANCE ($10K+) DAR 7-2003.14(b) (2) FAR 52.222-25	AFFIRMATIVE ACTION FOR VETS ($10K+) DAR 7-103.27 FAR 52.222-35	AFFIRMATIVE ACTION FOR HANDICAPPED ($2.5K+) DAR 7-103.28 FAR 52.222-36	CLEAN AIR AND WATER CERTIFICATE ($100K+) DAR 7-2003.71 FAR 52.223-1 & - 2	OVERSEAS DISTRIBUTION OF DEFENSE SUBCONTRACTS ($100K+) DAR 7-104.78 DOD FAR SUP 52.204 - 7005	REQUIRED (Y or N)	ADEQUATE (Y or N)	REQUIRED (Y or N)	ADEQUATE (Y or N)	REQUIRED (Y or N)	OBTAINED (Y or N)									
	69	70	71	72	73	74	75	76	77	78	79	80	81	82	83	84	85	86	87	88	89	90	91	
1																								1
2																								2
3																								3
4																								4
5																								5
6																								6
7																								7
8																								8
9																								9
10																								10
11																								11
12																								12
13																								13
14																								14
15																								15

AFSC FORM JUL 85 906 REPLACES AFCMD FORM 6, MAR 84, WHICH IS OBSOLETE.

PAGE 4 OF 4 PAGES

It has been estimated by the government that more than 80 percent of all procurements fall into the small purchases category, that is, those that are $25,000 or below. Thus, a simpler system should be established to handle these types of procurements simply and economically. Reducing the administrative costs means spending the minimum time and effort on each small purchase, but supplying complete and adequate documentation to justify each purchase. Figure 33 is one methodology that can be used.[35]

Small P.O. Justification Worksheet

Telephone Quotes ( )
Written Quotes ( )

RFP No. _____
REQ'N No. _____

Item No.	Qty.	Part/ Model	Description of Supplies/Services	Names of Bidders/Quoted Prices				
				1.	2.	3.	4.	5.
1.				$	$	$	$	$
2.								
3.								
4.								
5.								
6.								
7.								
8.								
9.								
10.								

Transportation Charges:
Total Vendor Quotation: $ | $ | $ | $ | $
Delivery ARO/Payment Terms:
Ship Via/FOB Point:
Socio-Economic Status:
Small (S), Large (L), Disadvantaged (D)
Woman-Owned (WO), Labor Surplus Area (LS)

| | S L D WO LS | S L D WO LS | S L D WO LS | S L D WO LS | S L D WO LS |

Competitive Source Selection Justification	Price Justification/Evaluation	Basis for PO. Award
Sole or Single (Preferred) Source Justification		
1. Only known source	1. Competitive quotation (See above competitive quotes)	1. Technical capability
1. Technically superior*	2. Catalog/published pricelist* GSA Federal Supply Schedule*	2. Fair and reasonable price
2. Only source meeting technical requirements	3. Established Market Price* Negotiated Price*	3. Acceptable delivery schedule
2. Low competitive bidder (See above competitive quotes)	4. Certification of price	4. Sole/single source award
3. Only source compatible with existing equipment	5. Comparison with prior purchase*	5. Competitive source selection
3. Only source meeting required delivery	6. Buyer's discretion (up to $10K)	6. Compatibility with existing equipment
4. Support services for existing vendor equipment	7. Blanket Purchase Agreement with qualified source (up to $10K)	7. Continuation of vendor furnished supplies/services
4. Compatibility with existing equipment	8.	8.
5. Continuation of vendor rental/lease equipment		
5. Continuation of vendor furnished supplies/services		
6. Customer preference*		
6. Proximity of source		
7. Buyer's choice (up to $5k) Reorder supplies/services		
7. Standard catalog item		
8.		

*Attach substantiation

Buyer: _____ Date: _____ P.O. No.: _____

Figure 33
Purchase Order Worksheet

Source Selection

Does the contractor have an adequate system for developing purchase requirements and source selection? Successful purchasing is based on formal planning and a key element is maximizing competition and a continuing effort to reduce sole source purchases. Liaison between technical and purchasing organizations on a continuing basis is necessary for competition procurements. Planning must include lead time consideration for schedule support. Criteria in the four areas of quality, price, performance, and facility capability must be carefully evaluated and considered when selecting the best vendor or subcontractor to keep your product on schedule and within cost. Use of different data systems (Figure 34) from different organizations and vendor evaluation visits by a multifuctional team is a must for an effective procurement system.

Vendor Evaluation -- Detail Weight

I. Quality

Weight

A. Quality personnel

	Weight
Very good--has a full, capable quality control staff	5
Good--has nearly a full quality control staff	4
Average--has a so-so quality control staff	3
Poor--has a limited quality control staff	2
Very poor--doesn't have any quality control staff	1

B. Quality policy and procedures

	Weight
Very good--has a corporate quality manual	5
Good--procedures for purchased material	4
Average--inspection procedures written	3
Poor--has some procedures written	2
Very poor--no quality procedures	1

C. Concern for quality

	Weight
Very good--quality concern at all stages	5
Good--raw material and in-process and finished goods stages	4
Average--raw material and finished goods stages	3
Poor--raw material or in-process or finished goods stages	2
Very poor--no inspection	1

D. History with company

	Weight
Very good--0-5% rate of nonconformity over last year	5
Good--6-10% rate of nonconformity over last year	4
Average--11-15% rate of nonconformity/no data	3
Poor--16-20% rate of nonconformity over last year	2
Very poor--21% or more rate of nonconformity	1

II. Pricing--Financial

Weight

A. Price--quality

	Weight
Very good--priced below competition/similar quality	5
Good--priced below most competition	4
Average--approximately same price as competition	3
Poor--priced above most competition	2
Very poor--priced above competition/similar quality	1

B. Price--negotiation/quote equals actual price

	Weight
Very good--never haggling/always meets quote	5
Good--seldom haggles	4
Average--sometimes haggles/usually meets quote	3
Poor--usually haggling	2
Very poor--always haggling/never meets quote	1

C. Financial ability

	Weight
Very good--profit-making enterprise	5
Good--slightly above breakeven	4
Average--breakeven ability/no data	3
Poor--less than breakeven	2
Very poor--financial loss	1

III. Performance

A. Technical performance (specifications)

	Weight
Very good--exceeds specifications/knows process	5
Good--sometimes above specifications	4
Average--runs at specifications	3
Poor--sometimes below specifications	2
Very poor--always below specifications/doesn't always understand process	1

Figure 34
Vendor Evaluation

Vendor Evaluation -- Detail Weight

	Weight
III. Performance (Cont'd)	
B. Delivery history	
Very good--always early	5
Good--mostly on time	4
Average--usually on time/ no data	3
Poor--seldom on time	2
Very poor--always late	1
C. Technical assistance (willingness to work with customers)	
Very good--high caliber/knows the process	5
Good--mostly helpful	4
Average--sometimes helpful	3
Poor--rarely helpful	2
Very poor--doesn't know the process	1
IV. Facilities capabilities	
A. Production capacity	
Very good--reserve production capabilities	5
Good--above requirements	4
Average--meets requirements	3
Poor--meets most of requirements	2
Very poor--cannot meet requirements	1
B. Manufacturing equipment	
Very good--up-to-date methods and equipment	5
Good--mostly modern plant/well-maintained	4
Average--so-so on methods and equipment	3
Poor--some new equipment	2
Very poor--old fashioned	1

Figure 34 (cont.)
Vendor Evaluation

General Dynamics and 3M use base systems to evaluate quality, price, performance, and facility capabilities. The areas are subdivided into 12 individual items. Quality fits into all areas but is most prevalent in the first five items. Quality is weighted between 40 and 60 percent of the total. Figure 35 shows a vendor rating form based on those four categories. If your company is already doing business with a prospective vendor, items like delivery history can be determined accurately without a visit to the vendor. Other points can be difficult to cover even in a visit, but a well-organized vendor will be prepared to explain its system to a prospective customer.[36]

Vendor Evaluation

Vendor _____

Location _____	**Rating***	**Comments**
I. Quality		
A. Quality Personnel	____	_____
B. Quality Procedure	____	_____
C. Concern for Quality	____	_____
D. Company History	____	_____
II. Price		
A. Price--Quality	____	_____
B. Price--Negotiation/Quote=Actual Price	____	_____
C. Financial Ability	____	_____
III. Performance		
A. Technical	____	_____
B. Delivery History	____	_____
C. Technical Assistance	____	_____
IV. Facility Capability		
A. Production Capacity	____	_____
B. Manufacturing Equipment	____	_____

Rated by: _____
Date: _____

Rating Scale*
5 Very Good
4 Good
3 Average
2 Poor
1 Very Poor
0 Negative

Figure 35
Vendor Evaluation Form

A scale of 0 to 5 is applied to each item, allowing for a quantified comparison among vendors. If no information is available, a 3 is given so the vendor is not disqualified or approved. The evaluation criteria should cover the following:

- Past performance including quality performance ratings.
- Financial position, general accounting methods, and cost controls.
- Product reliability.
- Management skills.
- Engineering and technical competency.
- Research and test facilities.
- Quality control (quality system survey and approval).
- Tooling capability.
- Manufacturing facilities.
- Production control capabilities.
- Transportation.
- Security.
- Manpower.
- Procurement system and subcontract management function.

See Figure 34 for a more detailed explanation of codes.

This sample vendor survey system applies quantified values to the estimated ability of vendors to supply at a consistently high level. A vendor survey is analogous to a profit and loss statement: it tells you what the status is at one point in time, but it will now guarantee what it will be at any other time. The communication started during the survey must continue for a good partnership to last a long time.

Cost and Price Analysis

Does the company have an adequate system for cost and price analysis that meets the criteria of Armed Services Pricing Manual 1; additionally, the subsequent negotiation should be accomplished in compliance with PL 87-654 and be fully documented covering rationale for decisions of pre- and post-negotiation positions. The contract award should be made only after a thorough review of the total package to ensure complete technical and contractual requirements are agreed on and included in the subcontract. The buyers should be required to establish negotiation objectives, which include the vendor evaluation scorecard (discussed previously) of quality, price, performance, and facility capabilities. The difference between the negotiation objectives and proposed settlement should be reviewed and approved by higher levels of management based on predetermined criteria for the different dollar thresholds of authority.

Subcontract Management

Does the company have an adequate documented system for managing subcontractors that provides visibility of cost, schedule, performance, and a means to validate subcontract status? During the postaward phase, subcontract management requires support, direction, and timely action by the prime contractor and a satisfactory relationship with the subcontractor. Reports, problem identification, problem solving, and the processing of subcontract changes are all evaluating factors.

Asking suppliers to meet contract requirements is one way to promote the timely receipt of quality goods and services. Showing them how to meet those objectives is a more effective way to guarantee their success and yours. Current supplier control techniques lean toward the first approach: using surveys, audits, source inspections, and frequent performance measurements to keep suppliers on target. A more innovative method adds sophisticated show-and-tell concepts to better educate and motivate suppliers in meeting your contract specifications. In short, telling them what kind of performance you expect and how you will help them improve will put you and your suppliers on a more cooperative level. This will serve you both in promoting higher productivity, continually improving product quality, and managing contracts more effectively.

An example of this method of procurement contract management was developed at General Dynamics Fort Worth manufacturing facility. It is here at Air Force Plant Four that General Dynamics produces the F-16 Multirole Fighter for the United States and several foreign military services. With a work force of 17,000 assembling more than 19,000 parts from 4,000 different suppliers, plant management cannot afford poor supplier performance. Fort Worth management developed its specialized approach to ensure the timely delivery of quality materials, parts, and services. The program, called Supplier Performance Evaluation Criteria (SPEC), combines communication, teamwork, and recognition concepts to promote more energetic contract compliance. The proper blending of these primary elements gives suppliers extra incentives for improving their performance.

Selling the Team Approach. Foremost in the SPEC program is the teamwork method of meeting contract objectives. Suppliers are consistently indoctrinated with the precept that their performance not only reflects on their own organization, but on the entire F-16 production team as well. Emphasis is placed upon General Dynamics' dedication to excellence. SPEC orientation features frequent references to the high level of quality attained by the Fort Worth division and its suppliers.

Using the Recognition Factor. Honoring superior achievement is another element of the SPEC system that induces suppliers to try harder. The Fort Worth division's Excellence Source Control program is used through SPEC as a tool to provide recognition. Suppliers who qualify are awarded with "designee" status under the Source Control program. Designee suppliers are those who have attained a consistently superior performance level in providing high-quality goods and services to the Fort Worth division. The award carries with it the delegation of specified quality assurance responsibilities, including the authorization of shipments in the absence of a procurement quality assurance representative from the Fort Worth division. Standards for gaining this level of excellence are high, and suppliers are constantly measured and encouraged to meet them.

Other means of recognition are used to promote better performance. Supplier commendations, award presentations, and promotions to designee status are continually publicized in Fort Worth's *Quality Assurance Bulletin* and other company publications. Formal awards presentations are conducted at supplier facilities to gain publicity and instill pride in supplier personnel.

The net gain from these recognition devices is to stimulate good suppliers to strive for consistent excellence while motivating average and low-performance suppliers to improve their position.

Telling Them How to Win. Communicating the program game plan and box score is what makes SPEC work. Suppliers are told in the earliest briefings what SPEC will do for them and what they must do to meet SPEC. The program gives suppliers information that is easily understood and free from misinterpretation. The following questions and answers are from an actual SPEC briefing:

Q: How will I be measured against General Dynamics Fort Worth division's standard of excellence?
A: All Fort Worth's costs associated with your product will be evaluated — from procurement through installation, checkout, and customer delivery. Minimal costs considered normal for an excellent supplier will be backed out of the cost equation.

Q: What are normal Fort Worth's costs for an excellent supplier?
A: Minimal sustaining effort, semiannual program reviews, periodic process and quality assurance system surveys, and annual audits.

Q: What costs are considered other than normal?
A: Costs due to late deliveries:
  • Out-of-station installations.
  • Producibility studies (if supplier design).
  • Increased quality assurance or subcontract management coverage at your facility.
  • Convening Material Review Boards at your facility.
  • Withholdings by our customer.

Costs due to less than excellent quality assurance performance:
  • Aircraft removal or replacements.
  • Reflights and ground aborts.
  • Stock purges.
  • Design changes (supplier responsible).
  • 100 percent or tightened sample inspections.
  • Flight tests.
  • Reinspection and retest.
  • Rework.
  • Corrective action investigations.
  • Laboratory tests and failure analysis.
  • Audits.

Q: How will you tell me my performance score?
A: Through periodic reports to your general manager.
  • Fort Worth's cost per $1,000 invoice price.
  • Fort Worth's total cost.
  • Cost equation element details.

Q: How will you use these reports?
A: Management will use them to communicate with supplier top management, aid in source selection, initiate cost recovery, and recognize supplier excellence. In addition, the information will be used for corporate-wide reporting and negotiating master procurement agreements.

Given this picture of SPEC program analysis and feedback, suppliers can readily see their position in the Fort Worth division procurement system. Their performance is measured on a bottom line of dollars. Former contract references to quality, corrective action, schedule impact, and acceptance levels are now translated into one simple equation based on the costs incurred by the Forth Worth division. Suppliers know specifically what their performance should equal. The quality of their products and services and the timeliness of their deliveries will be represented by the way they meet or exceed SPEC program procurement cost objectives.

For the supplier, the advantages of the SPEC program are obvious:
  • Measurement system helps improve operations.
  • High score opens door to repeat procurement.
  • Excellence status allows more flexible operation with less contractor surveillance.
  • Meeting SPEC gives the supplier a better position in the manufacturing marketplace.

For the General Dynamics Fort Worth division, a SPEC program offers greater benefits:
  • Reduced cost.
  • Clearer visibility of supplier performance.
  • Less reliance on costly audits and intensive corrective follow-up action.
  • Closer liaison with all supplier functions.
  • More positive performance evaluation technique.
  • Clearer picture for source selection.
  • More successful means for motivating suppliers.
  • More detailed identification of true procurement costs.

Fort Worth's experience in applying the SPEC program has proven successful. Supplier competition for excellence status is keen and growing. The ability to solve supplier problems more readily has also grown with the incorporation of SPEC program techniques. Moreover, the procurement cost control factor has improved in direct proportion to SPEC program success. What began as an innovative quality system is becoming a standard procurement contract management tool for General Dynamics. Although it doesn't replace standard procurement control techniques, such as surveys, audits and source inspections, it does help to make them more effective and less costly.[37]

Production and Manufacturing

The quantity production of a large system is an extremely complex task. No matter how much effort has gone into planning, major problems will occur because of the complexity of the manufacturing effort. As the manufacturing plans are implemented, a debugging phase will inevitably have to be undertaken whether it has been planned for or not. The need for this phase is generally not recognized.

Designing the manufacturing process for a large system rivals, and in many cases surpasses, the complexity of designing the system itself. Policy should require that this design of the manufacturing process be initiated early in the acquisition review process and culminate with a Production Readiness Review (PRR), which certifies that the program is ready to move into the production phase. The manufacturing design effort up to and including the PRR is primarily a paper exercise. The planning, reviews, assessments, and analyses made during this portion of the system acquisition process are in the form of paper reports. By the time of the PRR, some of the plans may have been converted to hardware in the form of a manufacturing line or system. But the point is, it is an unproven system, it only looks good on paper. There will always be the need for debugging the system. That requires time and money.

The deterministic process for designing the manufacturing system needs to be contrasted with the design process for the weapons system. This process is an iterative process with hardware tests required at the end of each phase to ensure that the system meets design requirements. Implicit in the design process is the expectation that deficiencies uncovered in the test at the end of one phase will be overcome in the next phase. If this level of effort is devoted to designing the system and the design effort of the manufacturing system is equal to it in magnitude and complexity, it follows that the design process for the manufacturing system should be comparable to the design process for the system. The reason often given for lack of a comparable manufacturing system design effort is cost. Solving the manufacturing system deficiencies of equipment inadequacies will require additional time and money. This will normally decrease the number of systems that can be procured. Again, costs increase because there is a loss in economy of scale. While it will normally be too expensive to design, build, and test a manufacturing system before production, more can be done to identify risks involved with the design of the manufacturing system and validating these risks through testing during development.

Manufacturing (production) is the conversion of raw materials into products and/or components thereof, through a series of manufacturing procedures and processes. It includes such major functions as manufacturing planning and scheduling, manufacturing engineering, fabrication and assembly, installation and checkout, demonstration and testing, product assurance, and determination of resource requirements.

Manufacturing management is the technique of planning, organizing, directing, coordinating, controlling, and monitoring the use of people, money, materials, equipment, and facilities to accomplish the manufacturing task economically. A manufacturing management system is composed essentially of planning, analysis, and control:[38]

- During the planning phase, consideration must be given to such factors as material acquisition, adequate labor force, engineering design, and provision for subcontractor support. Production feasibility and engineering design producibility are critical factors that must be considered early in a program. This consideration must include planning, new processes, facilities, tools and test equipment, and cost control during design.
- During the analysis phase, answers must be provided to such questions as: Is the manufacturing process working? Is it efficient? Is manufacturing being accomplished by the most economical method? Is the manufacturing plan being followed and are the established goals being met? During system design and development, these questions need to be projected into the future manufacturing effort to identify required preparatory actions and to assess risk levels.
- During the control phase, the manufacturing effort must be monitored to ensure that the manufacturing management technique functions are within the constraints and limits that have been established.

Accomplishing a stated manufacturing objective requires the manufacturing contractor to establish basic manufacturing policies, implement those policies through manufacturing procedures, and develop detailed manufacturing work instructions to attain the objective(s).

It is important for a manufacturing organization to be properly organized and to have the tasks completely assigned to effectively measure the performance against those tasks. Figure 36 shows a large aircraft manufacturing organization of approximately 8,000 employees. Measures of effectiveness for each of these areas should be established and performance tracked against the measure, to identify opportunities for improvement for the manufacturing organization. These measures typically fall into time, conformance, and cost measures of performance.

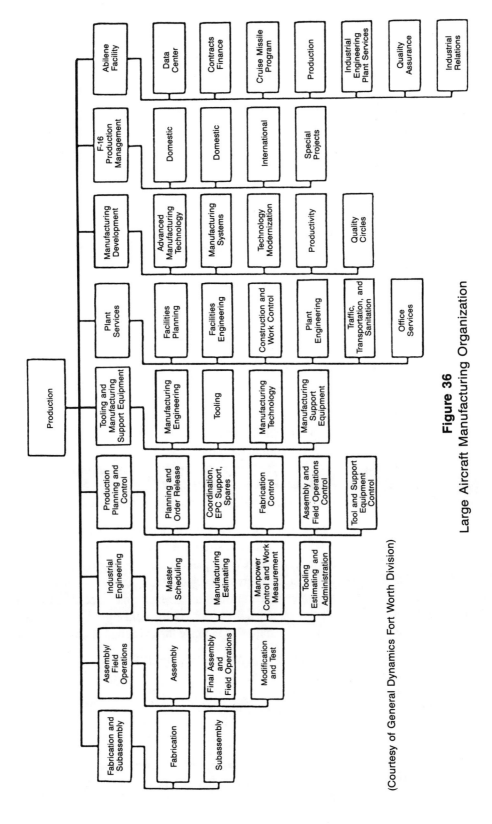

(Courtesy of General Dynamics Fort Worth Division)

Figure 36
Large Aircraft Manufacturing Organization

Authority and Responsibility

Are the authorities and responsibilities in the company's documented system for managing manufacturing operations complete, properly identified, assigned, and implemented? (See DAR 1-331, DAR 1-406, MIL-Q-9858A, MIL-STD-1528 [USAF], and MIL-STD-1567 [USAF].)

Time Measures. When a delivery schedule has been established, the effectiveness of the manufacturing organization in meeting that schedule should be evaluated. The delivery schedule should be integrated with deployment and training schedules and failure of the manufacturing organization to achieve and maintain schedule can have significant impact on customer sales and use. The company should establish some system to support projections of schedule attainment in future periods. This provides an opportunity to take actions to prevent delivery delays or minimize the impact of the delay on the deployment process. A useful tool for this future perspective is the line of balance technique.

Conformance Measures. When systems or equipments are presented for customer acceptance, it is generally assumed that they meet the technical requirements. Many times this assumption does not reflect reality. Equipment is presented accompanied by waiver and/or deviation requests (or approved waivers or deviations). There are also departures from technical documentation below the level of the customer's configuration control which are handled by material review board (MRB) action. In maintaining visibility of the conformance issue, some measures which could be of value are listed as follows:

- Number of waivers on completed units.
- Number of deviations on completed units.
- Open discrepancies passed from one station to the next in production — indicates future out-of-station work (Figure 37).
- MRB actions — probably as a ratio to direct manufacturing hours (Figure 38).

Cost Measures. Manufacturing cost is normally based on the assumption that the manufacture process will be relatively straightforward with operations being successfully accomplished as planned. Consequently, any deviation from this plan indicates the potential for cost problems. As such, the time and conformance measures above can give some indication of cost aberrations since there is normally a direct correlation between late delivery or conformance problems and cost. In addition, the following measures may also indicate the existence of cost problems.

- Yield rates on manufacturing operations (Figure 39).
- Percentage of out-of-station work.
- Engineering change volume.
- Scrap and rework rates (Figure 40).
- Reliability growth profiles.

These indicators do not replace normal management control systems but can be used as supplementary information or aid in predicting and isolating causative factors.

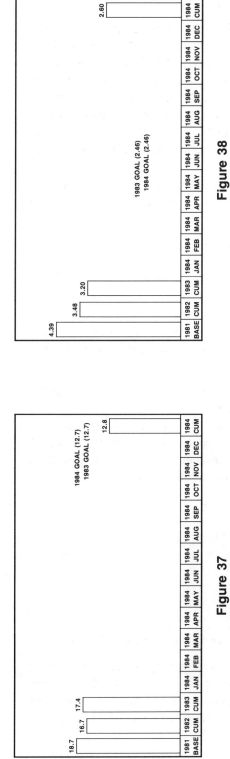

Figure 37

Percent Inspection Escapes

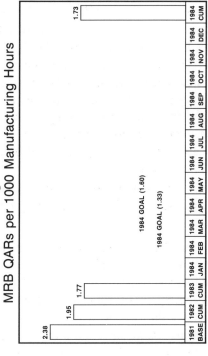

Figure 38

MRB QARs per 1000 Manufacturing Hours

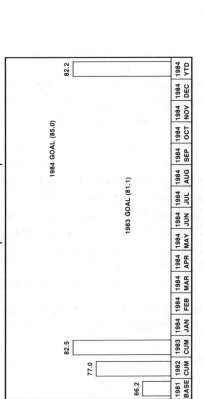

Figure 39

First Time Yield Acceptance Rates—
Machine Parts (Percent Accepted)

Figure 40

Percent Direct Labor Hours for Rework/Repair

Manufacturing Planning

Does the company have an adequate manufacturing planning system? (See DAR 1-406, DAR 15-205.21, DAR 25-101.1, DAR Appendix K, MIL-Q-9858A, and MIL-STD-1528 [USAF].) Manufacturing planning is concerned with intergrating people, materials, equipment, machine tools, and manufacturing processes identified by manufacturing engineering during production and design interface into the production of the end item. Manufacturing planning integrates program plans into master production plans, identifies critical paths of product flow, prepares flow plans, documents all required planning tasks, and adjusts manufacturing planning to changing work load demands.

The primary manufacturing planning challenge involves the evaluation of the qualitative measures of the manufacturing resources required for the production phase. Key guidelines are:

- Assuring that development contracts include requirements for contractor planning for production phase.
- Challenging assumptions concerning availability of manufacturing resources.
- Considering the risks inherent in the proposed approach and initiating actions to reduce the risk or provide fallback positions.
- Requiring contractor preparation of a manufacturing plan to assure that proper consideration has been given to the resource needs of the production phase and evaluating the plan.

Feasibility and Capability. The issues of manufacturing feasibility and capability are addressed initially in the product development process. The evaluation of manufacturing feasibility and capability is directed toward analysis of the compatibility of the manufacturing task and the facility and equipment required to accomplish it. The contractor's capability to successfully execute the manufacturing effort demands that the contractor (manufacturing source) has the following characteristics:

- An understanding of the manufacturing task.
- Adequate qualitative production skills.
- Sufficient personnel (on hand or available).
- Sufficient facility floor space.
- Equipment in satisfactory condition.
- Adequate, operable test equipment.
- Assured, capable suppliers.
- Management capability.
- A plan to integrate all resources into a cohesive manufacturing flow.

In the initial phases of product development, the program manager should ensure that a manufacturing feasibility assessment is done. The feasibility estimate determines the likelihood that a system design concept can be produced using existing manufacturing technology while simultaneously meeting quality, production rate, and cost requirements.

Demand Capacity Analysis. In developing a manufacturing plan, expected demands have to be analyzed in terms of equivalent resource requirements. Demand capacity analyses involve "exploding" units of output into equivalent units of input required to produce these outputs. The purpose is to define the amounts and types of materials and personnel skills that will be required to meet the contract requirements.

Some input resources remain fixed, whereas others are variable. Inputs such as machines, floor space, tools, and equipment — fixed capital assets — remain constant from one planning period to the next. Their availability is usually greater than needed. However, inputs such as personnel, materials, and supplies — working capital assets — are always changing. Their availability should be planned and controlled. Figure 41 shows the fixed and variable input resources required to produce products.

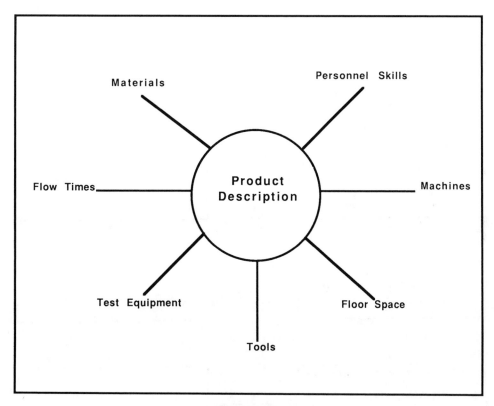

Figure 41
Fixed and Variable Resources

The planning strategy must be communicated to scheduling, with all the supporting information on work package size selection, content, manloading, work center level loading, facilities occupancy determinations, timing of actual material needs, process options in case tools and equipment are unavailable or overloaded, and many other considerations in the manufacturing plan. Since scheduling may be a function of several organizations or elements, this may be a problem area. Figure 42 illustrates the interrelationships between planning and scheduling in the shipbuilding industry.

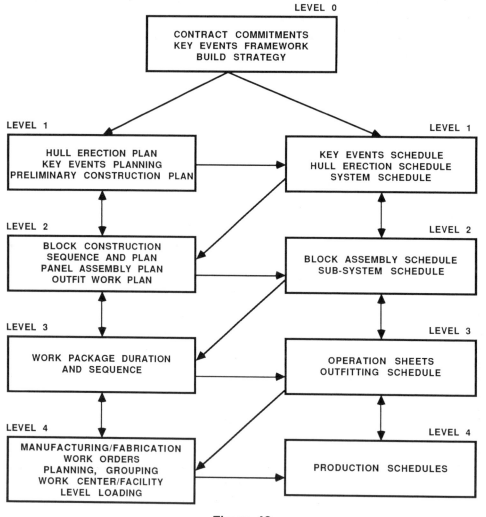

Figure 42
Planning and Scheduling

Part Three

Work Measurement Methods

Does manufacturing adequately use an integrated work measurement improvement system to control production costs and productivity? (See DAR 1-331, DAR 1-406, DAR 15, Part 2, and MIL-STD-1528 [USAF].)

Personnel is the company's most costly resource. An acceptable level of productivity requires an accurate measurement of work, use of optimum methods and processes, the establishment of productivity goals, and the identification and correction of problems preventing achievement of productivity goals.

Manufacturing Costs. As a result of continually increasing system cost coupled with relatively static fund availability, there is a need for program manager emphasis on the issue of system cost. Historically, cost has been viewed as a by-product of the development process. System technical performance parameters were made definite. Scheduled delivery dates were established. The cost factor, then, merely assured that performance was achieved within the contractual time constraints. In the current funding environment, there is a need to more fully evaluate and understand the element of program cost. To this end, specific management tools such as the C/SCSC and CPR have been developed and implemented to make cost integral to the system planning process. C/SCSC is the government methodology of tracking cost versus scheduled hours worked. It is defined by DOD Directive 7000.1. CPR (corrective performance reporting) is for contracts less than $10 million. These and others assist in controlling cost during the program life cycle.

Sources of Cost Growth. The experience of more than 30 major programs over an extended period of time gives some indication of the problems of cost growth most likely to beset new programs. These program histories show that the major factors contributing to cost growth and their approximate impact were:

- Changes in Cost Estimates — Refinements of the base program estimate accounted for 12 percent of the total cost growth.
- Engineering Changes — Alterations in physical or functional characteristics were 20 percent.
- Schedule Changes — Changes in delivery schedules or program milestones were 15 percent.
- Economic Changes — Escalation adjustments in contracts and other changes in the purchasing power of the dollar were 30 percent. Inflation over the past few years would increase this percentage.
- Support Changes — Changes in spare parts, training, testing, and other support requirements were 7 percent.

A variety of other items made up the balance of some 8 percent of the total cost growth in these programs.[39]

Estimates Based on Engineered Standards. Engineered standards are useful for developing cost estimates once there is a clear definition of the detailed system configuration. Engineered standards are those developed using a recognized technique such as time study, work sampling, standard data, or a recognized predetermined time system. These standards provide the benefit of detail description of required manufacturing operations and provide a baseline for the evaluation of actual incurred costs (Figure 43).

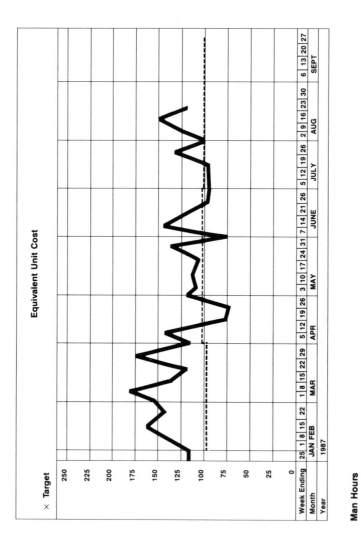

Figure 43
Engineering Standards

Industrial Engineering Standards (IES). IES define and measure, in unit man hours or dollars, the work content of the discrete tasks to be performed in accomplishing a given operation or producing an item. IES represent average skills, times, and rates. These standards are used primarily to estimate contractor functional costs such as engineering, tooling, manufacturing, and product assurance.

IES are developed as follows:

- A work statement, set of drawings, or specification is received or developed.
- Each engineering or production operation required to produce the item or accomplish the designated task is specified.
- The work stations where each operation will be performed are designated.
- The kinds of labor and material required to produce the item or accomplish the operation are given in detail. Tooling requirements are identified with man-hour and material estimates.
- IES studies are conducted to determine the most economical method of performing each manufacturing operation.
- An estimated time standard for performing each task is established using time and motion studies or predetermined time systems plus experience in performing similar tasks.
- Labor standards for specific operations may be combined to provide a labor standard for a component, subassembly, major equipment, or subsystem. Standards may also be developed to cover waste, rework, tooling, and engineering.
- Labor efficiency factors are used to adjust standard labor hours to actual labor hours. In general, labor efficiency, utilization, or effectiveness measures represent the ratio of standard hours planned to the actual hours expended for a given work operation.
- Periodically, time standards are adjusted to reflect changes in production methods. Over a period of years some standards become stabilized to such an extent that they become plant, product, or industry standards.

Workload Control

Does the company have an adequate system for forecasting, scheduling, and controlling workloads? (See DAR 1-331, DAR 1-406, DAR 1-903, DAR 1-905, DAR-25-101.1, DAR Appendix K, and MIL-STD-1528 [USAF].) Detailed scheduling predetermines, then systematically distributes and releases workloads to manufacturing shops according to known manpower, material, and equipment capabilities. The schedule allocates personnel resources and material into a daily time frame, which includes a start and finish time. It includes routing, dispatching, and expediting for storage, control, and protection of "in-process" inventories and assurance that work is done as scheduled.

Master-Phasing Schedule. The master-phasing schedule establishes the basic relationship between engineering release, parts and material, procurement, design release, fabrication, assembly, installation, test, product assurance, and delivery of product. It summarizes the program to ensure compatibility of all subsequent planning and scheduling. The master-phasing schedule is developed to reflect both the program requirements and contractor commitments. Completion milestone dates are normally displayed pictorially in a master-phasing chart, which visually depicts milestones for each major phase and planning element that must be completed. Figure 44 lists the major events for which schedule relationships are required in a typical defense system production program.

Events

Program Milestones

Program go-ahead
Long-lead go-ahead
Manufacturing decision
Start design layouts
Engineering drawing release
Contract delivery schedules

Associate Contractors

Subsystems on-dock

Fabrication, Assembly, and Checkout

Schedules and events

Operations Scheduling

Issue assembly plan
Issue final tooling plan
Issue master schedule

Purchasing/Major Subcontracts

Make-or-buy plan
Purchase order awards
Major system awards
Procure long-lead material
PRR's for critical major subcontracts

Qualification Testing

Components
Subsystems
Systems

Manufacturing and Engineering

Technology development plan
Subcontract data packages
Manufacturing tooling policy
Manufacturing or purchasing plan
Producibility studies
Identify rate tooling

Tooling

Fabricate master tools
Fabricate detail tooling
Fabricate assembly tooling
Design tooling
Design interface tooling in
  support of subcontractors
Fabricate manufacturing tooling

Schedule

(Show appropriate start and completion dates by months or weeks in this section of the schedule.)

Figure 44
Major Events Schedule for a
Typical Defense System Acquisition Program (Simplified)

Events	Schedule
Facilities	(Show appropriate start and completion dates by months or weeks in this section of the schedule.)
Manufacturing station plan	
Layouts for facilities	
Facility contracts extensions	
Design, contract, prepare, and	
occupy manufacturing facilities	
Set up assembly areas for manufacturing	
Manpower	
Develop training plan	
Acquire personnel	
Train personnel	
Management Systems	
Issue material requirements system	
Issue material procurement and	
inventory system	
Issue production control system	
Issue work measurement system	

Figure 44 (cont.)
Major Events Schedule for a
Typical Defense System Acquisition Program (Simplified)

The master-phasing schedule provides the basic schedule framework within which detailed schedule planning is accomplished. The master-phasing schedule is used to develop the first unit flow chart, master schedules, and overall schedule direction for the various functional organizations. Figure 45 shows a typical hierarchy of schedules.

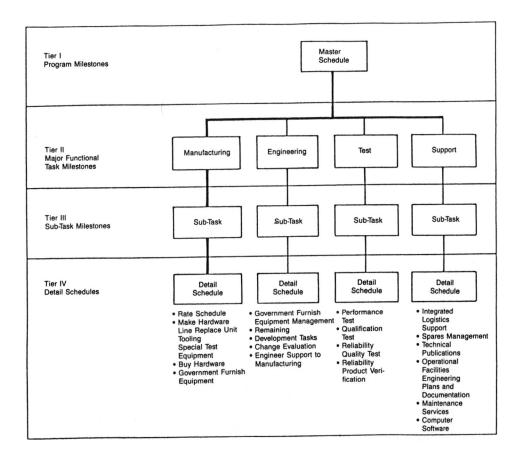

Figure 45
Typical Hierarchy of Schedules

With the overall sequence of the major operations defined, all of the simultaneous activities and operations must be scheduled for completion to meet subsequent events dependent on them. Correspondingly, start times for all the activities and operations being carried on simultaneously are determined in turn by individually working back through their allowable flow times. Thus, even though many separate assemblies needed to make up one larger assembly may have various flow times, they will all be scheduled to complete at the same time. After this, their individual flow times will dictate the scheduling of their starting dates.

In this manner, the entire schedule can be displayed on one chart for the first production unit. The phasing of all operations and activities is neatly and simply controlled despite the complexities of the interrelationships. All organizations can determine at a glance when their responsibilities start, how low they are to carry them out, and when they must be completed.

Master Schedules. Master schedules are developed in a manner similar to the first unit flow chart except that they show all production components or units sequentially over a period of time instead of just the first unit. Master schedules are so called because they are the major control for overall manufacturing operations. They are the basis for coordinating all supporting elements of a program from space and facilities requirements to tooling and equipment, vendor activity, labor, raw material preparation, detail parts fabrication, assembly and installation operations, functional testing, and finally, delivery to the customer. Figure 46 shows a typical master schedule for an electronics system showing span times for specific units from procurement to delivery.

Part Three

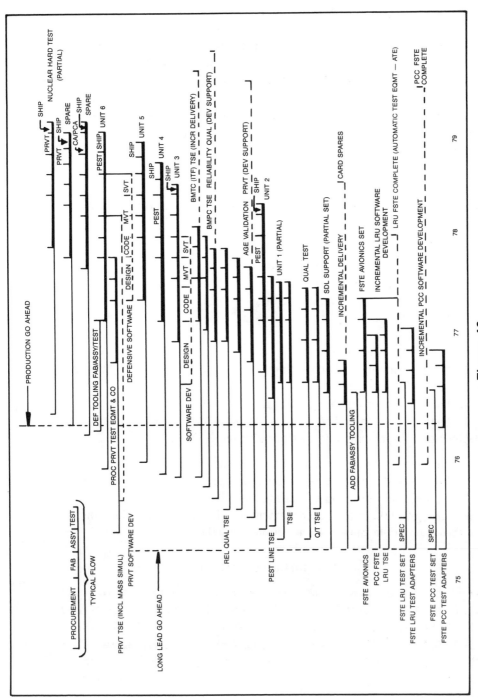

Figure 46
Master Schedule

111

Learning Improvement. The learning curve was adapted from the historical observation that individuals performing repetitive tasks exhibit an improvement in performance as the task is repeated a number of times. Empirical studies of this phenomenon yielded three conclusions on which the current theory and practice is based. For a constant rate: the time required to perform a task reduces as the task is repeated; the amount of improvement decreases as more units are produced; and, the rate of improvement has sufficient consistency to allow its use as a prediction tool.

The consistency in improvement has been found to exist in the form of a constant percentage reduction in time required over successively doubled quantities of units produced.

By its title, the learning curve focuses attention on the worker learning the job. This is just one of the components contributing to the reduction in time requirements. The following elements contribute to total manufacturing improvement:

- Worker learner.
- Supervisory learning.
- Reductions in crowded work stations.
- Tooling improvements.
- Design producibility improvements.
- Reduced engineering liaison.
- Improved work methods.
- Reduced parts shortages.
- Improved planning and scheduling.
- Increased lot sizes.
- Reduced engineering change activity.
- Reduction in scrap and rework.
- Operation sequencing and synchronization.

Total improvement is a combination of personnel learning and management action. While some studies have been done, there are no general observations that can be made concerning the relative contribution of the specific elements. The critical issue is to recognize the role of management in achieving these reductions and to ensure that appropriate management actions are taken.

Transportation System

Does the company have an adequate packaging, handling, and transporting system? (See DAR 3-809, 49 CFR, MIL-STD-648, MIL-STD-794, MIL-STD-834, MIL-STD-881, MIL-STD-1365, MIL-STD-1366, MIL-STD-1367, MIL-STD-1510, MIL-P-9024, MIL-A-8421, MIL-Q-9858A, and AFSC Design Handbook 1-11.) Getting the materials in from the vendors and completing the manufacturing task is rigorous and is not completed until the finished product is packaged and shipped to the distribution centers or customers. The product should be shipped economically in the correct quantity to the correct location. It should arrive undamaged and be a zero discrepancy product. All paperwork, invoices, certification, and test reports should be included.

The company's procedures should allow the necessary transportability and packaging interfaces with design, manufacturing, and transportation. The procedures and analyses should consider the packaging costs, personnel resources versus workload and personnel skill levels versus need, packaging data controls and testing, and specifications for the company and the vendor.

Shipping and Receiving. Inspection records at several companies were reviewed and analyzed. Several areas of interest and concern were noted in the receiving of materials coming in from vendors, and the products, kits, and parts going out to customers. These include the following:

- Invoices.
- Certification and test results.
- Out-of-date or spoiled time-sensitive materials.
- Inadequate packaging damage.
- Components failure during functional test.
- Wrong parts.
- Incomplete kits.
- Product marking errors or omissions.

The cost of returning the product to vendors or correcting all of these anomalies is high. These areas should have productivity measures similar to those for the production line.

Logistics and Customer Support

The customer has to be considered the most important part of the development, design, manufacturing, and field service of any company's product cycle. As Gen. Omar N. Bradley said in *A General's Life:*

> "This is the dullest subject in the world, and no writer has ever succeeded in glamorizing it. The result is that logistics are usually either down played or ignored altogether. But logistics were the lifeblood of the Allied armies in France. Without ports and facilities we could not supply our armies. We could not move, shoot, eat, land new troops, or evacuate the wounded."

This is equally true in not only the military environment, but any commercial enterprise. There must be a unified and iterative approach to the management and technical activities necessary to: (1) cause support considerations to influence both requirements and design, (2) define support requirements that are optimally related to the design and to each other, (3) acquire the required support, and (4) provide for the required support in the operational phase at minimum cost.

Part Three

Integrated Logistics

Does the company have an adequate integrated logistics support management system? (See AFR 800-0, AFLC/AFSCP 800-34, and DOD 5000.39.) An adequate management system for integrated logistics support (ILS) provides both management functions and technical effort to integrate logistics considerations and logistics planning into the design process and supportabilities of systems, equipments, and modification programs. The logistics support elements of the following are integrated with each other into a total system:

- Reliability and maintainability interface.
- Maintenance planning.
- Support equipment.
- Supply support.
- Packaging, handling, and transportation.
- Technical data.
- Facilities.
- Manpower requirements and personnel.
- Training and training support.
- Logistics support resource funds.
- Logistics support management information.
- Computer resources support.
- Energy management.
- Survivability.
- ILS test and evaluation.

When the baseline of any one logistics element is changed or proposed to be changed, the effect on all other logistics elements and on the total system is formally considered and necessary adjustments are made. The management system established should achieve the coordination required in integrating the multidiscipline objectives of logistics and customer support.

The development of any system, whether in the DOD or commercial enterprise, should follow some methical process to plan the management and technical tasks. A typical DOD process is shown in Figure 47.

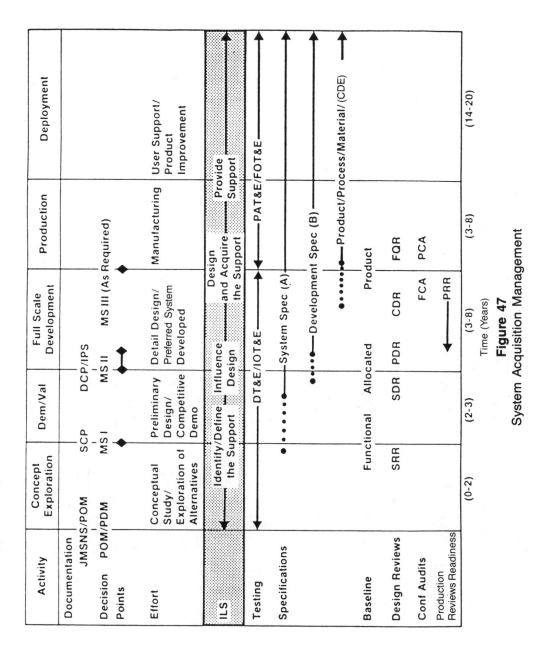

Figure 47

System Acquisition Management

The Integrated Logistics Support Process

Concept Exploration	Demonstration and Validation	Full-Scale Development	Production and Deployment
• Identify Logistics Constraints	• Investigation/ Demonstration of Alternatives	• Prototype Development of Selected Alternative	• Quantity Production of System and Its Requisite Support
• Investigate Lessons Learned	• Cost and Operational Effectiveness Analysis	• Trade-Off Process Within Selected Alternative	• Concurrent Fielding of System and All Requisite ILS
• Invent Acquisition Logistics Strategy	• Identification of Required Support	• Refine ILS Plan	• Post Production Support
• Tailor Elements of ILS	• Prepare ILS	• Conduct LSA	
• ILS Analyses	• ILS Analyses	• Acquire and Test ILS	

MILESTONE I — MILESTONE II — MILESTONE III

• Program initiated
• Identify system alternatives

• Program refined
• Evaluate system alternatives

• Tentative decision to produce and deploy the selected system alternative

• Firm decision to produce and deploy

System Acquisition Phase Scale

System Acquisition Phase	Concept Exploration	Demo/ Valid	FSD	Production	Operation and Support

Figure 48
System Acquisition Process

Logistics Plan

Does the company have a logistics plan to meet the needs of the product program? The support process should identify the various activities that need to be considered and acted upon during the concept exploration. These major activities shown in Figure 48 should be started with an adequate organization to fully analyze and develop the concepts and basic organizations and parametric costs. Some typical analyses, data, and materials and surveys are shown in Figure 49.

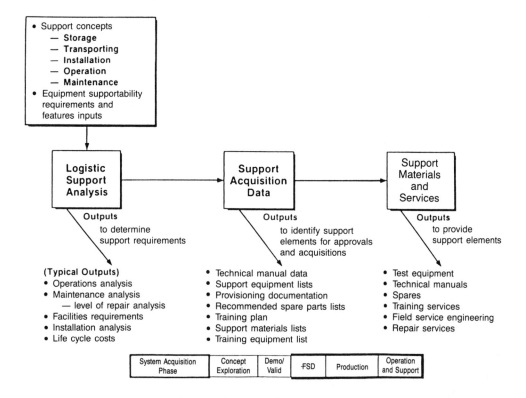

Figure 49
ILS Support Acquisition Process

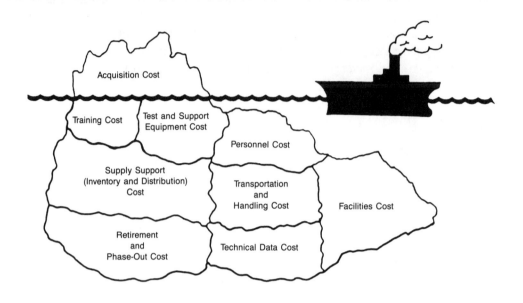

Figure 50
Support Costs

Staffing

Does the company have an adequate organization and staff to accomplish the logistics and customer support service? It is important to the company that the logistics responsibilities for fielding an airplane, an automobile, a refrigerator, a line of tires, etc., be considered because the cost of designing and manufacturing the product is probably only one tenth of the total program costs. If the support costs are not adequately considered (Figure 50), customer dissatisfaction can bankrupt the firm.

A typical logistics organization is shown in Figure 51.

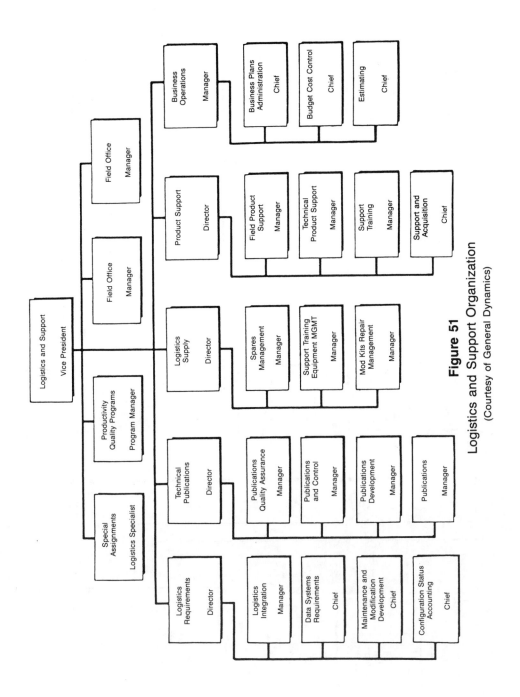

Figure 51

Logistics and Support Organization
(Courtesy of General Dynamics)

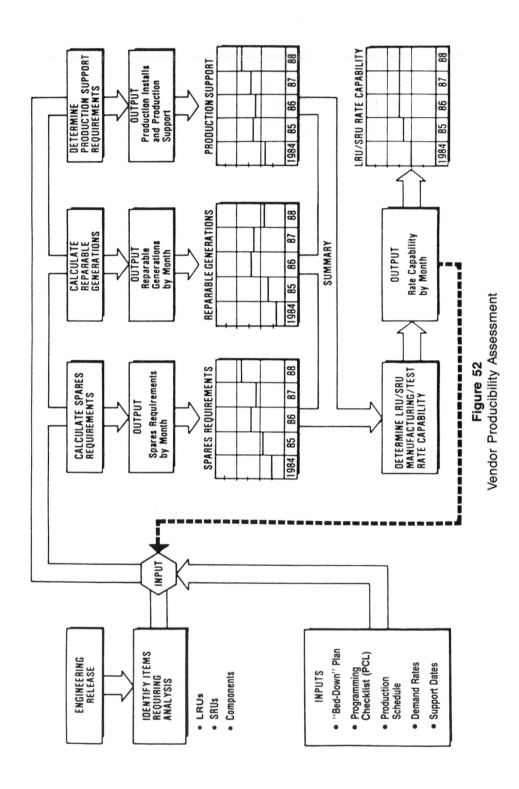

Figure 52
Vendor Producibility Assessment

Logistics requirements director carries out the planning:

• Assures system is designed for supportability.
• Develops integrated support plan.
• Develops and selects alternatives as required.

Business operations manager carries out the organization:

• Assembly resources required to carry out plan.
  - Personnel
  - Budget

Logistics supply director carries out the coordination:

• Ensures harmony among ILS elements.
• Assures high level of integration between contractor and customer.

Product support director carries out the direction:

• Provides guidance to all ILS functions.
  - What
  - When
  - Who

The productivity quality program manager carries out the controlling:

• Establishes information feedback network.
  - Plan
  - Means of measurement
  - Corrective action mechanism

Vendor's Role

Has the company adequately assessed the vendor's role in the logistics lifeline? Most products of any complexity are assembled and produced using 50 to 70 percent by part count from a vendor base, according to research compiled by the author during 1975 to 1985. Figure 52 shows a typical vendor producibility assessment flow.

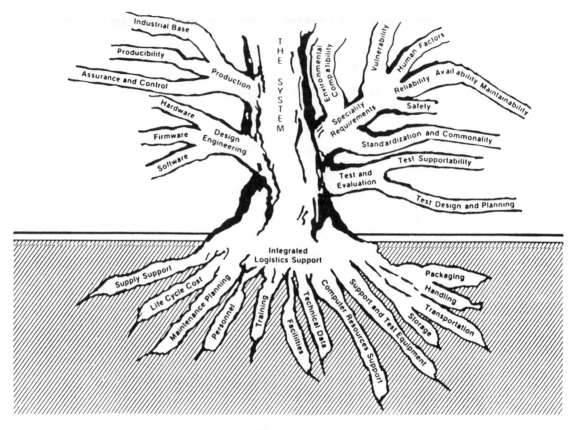

Figure 53
Logistics Support — Lifeline of the Product

Marketing and Planning

The marketing function is more difficult to evaluate by the MAP than other functional departments. Marketing and planning for sales are more dependent on external influences, such as market prices, general trends of the economy, and national and international inflation, than are the other functions. As covered in *General Management*, page 18, strategic and operating plans lay out the basic framework of operation.

Part Three

Marketing Planning Efforts

Are marketing management efforts directed to accomplishing the strategic and operating plans? The primary emphasis should be on creative market segmentation, efficient R&D expenditures, controlled growth, and strong leadership. These dimensions of market environment and competitive strategy (Figure 54) should be closely analyzed. Policies should be developed for each and action should be taken to exploit the areas dictated by strategic and operating plans.[40]

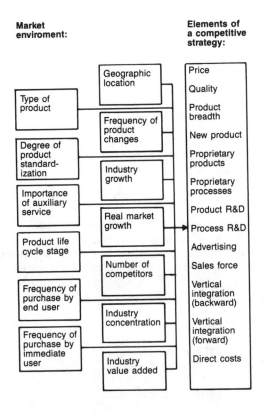

Figure 54
Dimensions of Market Environment
and Competitive Strategy

Market Research

Is market research management capable of dynamic tactics during the products life cycle? As a product moves through the stages of its life cycle, it places major strains on different parts of the industry infrastructure. One result of these pressures is the creation of highly challenging opportunities for decisive preemption, in which the firm achieves a sustained period of advantage over its competitors. Such preemptions can determine the destiny of an entire industry (Figure 55).

Supply Systems

1. Secure access to raw materials or components.
2. Preempt production equipment.
3. Dominate supply logistics.

Product or Service

1. Introduce new product lines.
2. Develop dominant product design.
3. Position product more effectively.
4. Secure accelerated approval from agencies.
5. Acquire product development and delivery skills.
6. Expand scope of product.

Production Systems

1. Develop proprietary production methods.
2. Expand capacity aggressively.
3. Attempt vertical integration with key suppliers.
4. Secure scarce and critical production skills.

Customers

1. Segment market.
2. Develop early brand awareness.
3. Educate customers in usage skills.
4. Capture key accounts.

Distribution and Service Systems

1. Occupy prime locations.
2. Develop preferential access to key distributors.
3. Control distribution logistics.
4. Ensure access to superior service systems.
5. Develop distributor skills.

Figure 55
Preemptive Opportunities

The strategist seeks opportunities to upset industry equilibrium. One weapon that the strategist uses to secure an advantage over competitors is the preemptive move. It is a tactic that enables the strategist's firm to disrupt the "normal" course of industry events so as to develop new conditions that will work to the disadvantage of competing companies.

A preemptive move is a major action taken by a company before its adversaries can make similar or forestalling moves. That action allows the company to secure an advantageous position from which its competitors cannot easily dislodge it.

Preemptive Strategy Guidelines. A company that wishes to design a preemptive move must do four things:

1. Analyze the industry chain to identify emerging opportunities to exploit those links where competitors are weak or have made little commitment — or where their strengths have resulted in a critical lack of flexibility.
2. Recognize that to be effective, preemptive moves need not occupy *all* positions, nor need they preempt *all* competitors. It is sufficient to select any emerging opportunities that affect enough competitors for long enough to make a material difference in the industry.
3. Recognize that preemptive moves cannot be made without some risk. Calculated risks must be taken, and the extent to which a particular preemptive action can be reversed, if necessary, increases its attractiveness.
4. Recognize that the benefits of preemptive moves are not permanent; competitors *will* respond. Hence, it is important to seek moves that can be implemented rapidly but will serve to delay response by competing firms. What should be considered in predicting competitors' responses is the extent to which an appropriate response by competing companies will cannibalize their existing products; threaten their major investments in supply, production, distribution, or service systems; challenge their images, traditions, or major strategic thrusts; or antagonize powerful third parties with a vested interest in the competitors' response. In these ways, aggressive companies can preemptively seize industry leadership from their competitors.[41]

Long-Range Quotas

Are long-range sales quotas established for: (1) products or product lines, (2) sales or geographic areas, and (3) salespersons? The ability of a sales organization to perform its assigned tasks has to be evaluated. Sales managers must not only meet quotas that should result in a profitable operation, but they should also be scored on their ability to increase customer satisfaction, meet changing business conditions, and motivate their sales force (low turnover and high unit output).

Advertising

Is advertising management capable of developing a well-thought-out and well-integrated advertising program? The areas that should receive high attention are:

(1) the advertising budget, (2) the tie-in of regular and special promotions to advertising for the product lines, (3) the competency of advertising management to meet current sales objectives during savings of the economy, and (4) the ability to operate effectively within the set budgets. Finally, is the organization an innovator in product and service advertising as proven by customer and marketing surveys?

Physical Distribution

Is the physical distribution an integral part of long-range marketing plans? It does no good to establish a plan to turn out a viable product in large quantities unless the distribution centers are located in the marketing areas. The value received for cost incurred is a key determining factor, after customer service and satisfaction. Again, customer cost benefits and the rate of inventory turnover should be addressed in the distribution analysis and plan.

Contracts and Estimating

A company's contract and estimating system covers those elements related to the negotiation of contracts, estimating practices, settlements of terminations, compensation structure principles on reimbursements, formalization of informal commitments, compliance with formal directions from a contracting officer, and fulfillment of contractual terms and conditions. The contractor may carry out the overall function of contract administration in various functional departments throughout its organizational structure. It is essential that the contractor identify and specify the delegated authority and responsibility of the specific element performing its aspect of the contract administration function.

Authority and Responsibility

Are the authorities and responsibilities in the contractor's documented contract administration system complete, properly identified, assigned, and implemented? In the arena of increasing government regulation and more specifications and external audits, it is imperative that close attention be given to all elements of the system. (See DAR 1.331 and 1-903.) The documented system should cover most, if not all, of the following arsenal of weapons the DOD has to influence costs with its customers:

- Cost Monitoring Reviews
- Procurement System Approval
- Forward Pricing Rate Recommendations and Agreements
- Final Rate Settlements
- Proposal Evaluations
- Compensation Review
- Cost and Schedule Control System Criteria Reviews
- Should Cost Reviews
- Cost Avoidance Notices

- Cost Accounting Standard Adjustments
- Costs in Defective Pricing Adjustments
- Contract Modification Negotiations
- Termination Settlement Negotiations
- Disputes
- Equal Employment Opportunity Compliance Reviews
- Total Quality Systems Approval Withdrawals
- Material Review Board System Approval Withdrawals
- Corrective Action Systems Approval Withdrawals
- Supplier Quality Assurance System Approval Withdrawals
- Contractor Self-Insurance Approvals
- Group Insurance Plan Approvals
- Audits
- Withholding Payments
- Contractor Procurement System Approvals
- Contractor Property System Approvals
- Purchase Order Reviews
- Preaward Surveys
- Determination of Liability for Property Damage
- Hazard Reports
- SAFE-ALERTS
- Suspension Air Force Quality Assurance
- Air Force Deficiency Reporting
- Productivity Progress
- Energy Conservation Programs
- Work Measurement
- Disposal of Government Property
- Maximum Acceptable Utilization Reviews of Government Property
- Data Management
- Program Management Reviews
- Make of Buy Analysis
- Determination of Special Test Equipment
- Air Force Suggestion Program
- Fraud, Waste, and Abuse Program

Estimating System

Does the company have an estimating system that provides accurate, complete, and timely price proposals? (See PL 91-379, DAR 7-104.83, 7-202.4, 3-506, 3-807.2, 3-809[c], 16-206, and ASPM #1.) The company's estimating system should be set up to time phase all cost proposals in work to meet the customers deadlines, including computer software and software resources when applicable. As noted earlier, a productivity or quality improvement program parameter should be established to track proposal responsiveness (Figure 56). Either your government customer has a parameter that you will be measured against, or you should have one internally to service your commercial customer efficiently.

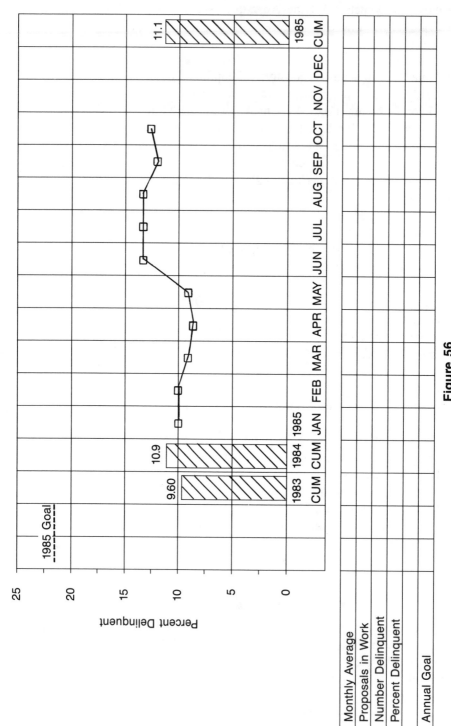

Figure 56

Quality Improvement Program Percent Proposals
Delinquent to Schedule Contracts and Estimating

When proposals are not handled in a timely manner, the impact of late turn-ons to engineering, manufacturing, and procurement can be devastating to product quality and to meeting the customers' schedules and desires.

Overhead Pricing Rates

Does the company have an adequate system for ensuring that overhead forward pricing rate agreement (FPRA) proposals and final overhead claims are timely and responsive? (See DAR 7-204.16, 3-807.3, and 3-807.12.) Timely submission of overhead claims rate proposals and claims for forward pricing and final settlements are of utmost importance to expedite negotiation of new contractual effort and closure of completed contracts. Using overhead FPRAs facilitates pricing procurement actions negotiated by both the buying organizations and the detachments. Settling final overhead rates is a key step in closing out government cost-type contracts. The negotiated final overhead rates clause requires contractors to submit final claims no later than 90 days after the close of the contractor fiscal year.

In large divisions or companies that negotiate proposals by the hundreds each month, FPRAs are a smart way of doing business. If FPRAs and parametric estimating are used together the efficiency of turning around proposals can be improved tenfold. However, the government and other large customers also have to use innovative ways to accomplish the technical and cost analysis on your proposals. Otherwise the time frames of the proposal limits will be exceeded and the proposal has to be updated. Combine this with major subcontractor attachments and the system gets stagnated and continuous reworks of proposals become time consuming.

Administrative Requirements

Does the company have a system for managing the various administrative requirements imposed by the recurring requirements of government contracts? (See DAR 7-103.2, 7-103.7, 7-104.86, 7-104.35, 7-108.1, 7-203.4, 7-104.4, 7-104.51, 7-104.28, 7-203.3, 16-815, 1-902, DAR APP E, AFSCR 310-1 and AFP 70-22.) Government contracts carry with them numerous administrative and reporting requirements. A common feature of these requirements is that they require interaction between the company contract administration function and the government contract administration activity. Frequently, the company contacts the government because of unexpected events or at irregular intervals. At the same time, many administrative requirements affect more than one aspect of the company's operations, and the company's internal communication is important. An orderly, integrated, systematic set of instructions helps to ensure that complete, correctly documented, timely notification is given to all by appropriate parties.

Many studies have been done in the DOD by the author. The failure to centrally manage, within a division or company, has resulted in proliferation and duplication with unnecessary cost increases. What can be learned from history?

Symptoms of basic deficiencies:

- No central review or control of internal or external reporting requirements.
- Duplication of reports.
- No formal reports control program.
- No current inventory of reports.
- No accounting of individual report costs.
- No periodic evaluation of individual report need and use versus cost.
- No central forms control activity.

Fundamental causes:

- Reports producing group functions as service organization with no responsibility to make management evaluations.
- Management not aware of man-hour or dollar costs of total reports, or extent of duplication.

Actions to be taken:

- Central reports and forms control group established.
- Mandatory approval for new reports.
- Complete, updated report inventory.
- Accounting procedures altered to produce costs of individual reports.
- Formal reports established for control and reduction program.
- Requirement for periodic economic justification of existing reports and tab runs.

Termination Settlements

Does the company have an adequate system for settlement of terminated contracts/subcontracts? (See DAR 7-301.21, 7-203.10, 8-303, 8-304, 8-406, 24-202, and 24.203.) Prompt and effective settlement of terminated contracts permits: (1) early release of excess contract funds that can be used on other contracts; (2) excess government property to be transferred to other contracts, returned to a depot, or disposed of through surplus sales; (3) reduction of settlement expenses; (4) elimination of costs of maintaining open docket files; and perhaps the most important, (5) allows the company to be paid for its termination costs. History is a great predictor of the future.

Symptoms of basic deficiencies:

- Work stoppage (including subcontractors) as directed by the termination notice.
- Lack of control and aggressive follow-up by the buyer.
- Subcontractor claims not settled promptly.
- Increased subcontract termination costs.
- Delays by buyers in updating purchase order files before forwarding to termination coordinator.
- Delayed transmittal of termination notice.
- Delayed subcontractor notification.

Fundamental causes:

- Lack of managerial emphasis on the termination function.
- Contractor decentralization of the termination function combined with lack of standardized procedures.
- Delay by the customer in requesting audit assistance.
- Auditing a claim.

Actions to be taken:

- Standardized terminations policies.
- Revised procedures to provide quicker response on termination notices.
- Procedures that provide instructions to subcontractors immediately after termination notice.
- Regular top management review of termination status.
- Electronic data processing or computerized system to reduce flow time of paperwork in material control areas.

Industrial Property Management

A company usually has a large part of its assets in industrial property. Top management pays close attention to cash flow, receivables, and inventories, but should pay more attention to the accountability and control of property, especially government property.

The company should control, protect, preserve, and maintain all property in its possession. The company's policies and procedures should clearly delineate the responsibilities for controlling each type of government asset and provide authority to carry out those responsibilities. The contractor property control system should provide for feedback of information between operating divisions and top property management personnel, and for monitoring compliance with documented policies and procedures. The contractor should also take prompt corrective action when any portion of its property control system is found inadequate by a customer.

A guideline for establishing a property control system is the Defense Acquisition Regulation Appendix B-101.

Authority and Responsibility

Are the authorities and responsibilities in the company's documented system for managing property complete, properly identified, assigned, and implemented? (See DAR APP B-101, 203, 311, 603, and DAR 7-104.28.) A typical system should address accountability, inventory, and disposition of the various types of property in accordance with the DOD and Internal Revenue System procedures. That typical system should follow a logical sequence (Figure 57).

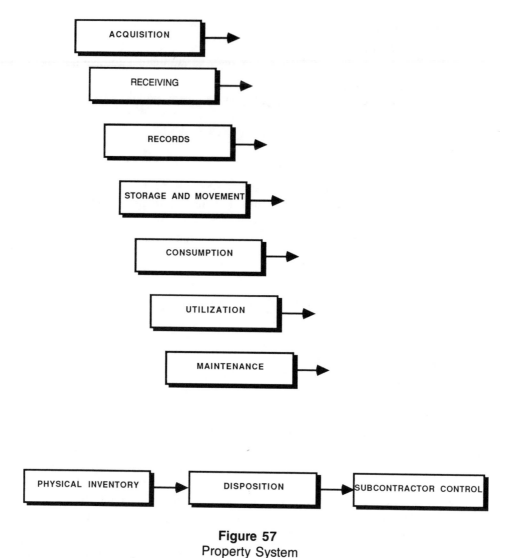

Figure 57
Property System

In the world of government contracting the management of government furnished property can be challenging. At the last count, government furnished property totaling $22 billion was in the hands of defense contractors. Effective contracting and control requires an understanding of not only the types of GFP, but also the many policies concerning their use.[42]

Facilities. Facilities are defined as industrial property for production, repair, maintenance, test, or evaluation. Facilities are further classified as real estate — buildings or property; industrial plant equipment — machines that cut, abrade, and shape, and that are of high dollar value; and other plant equipment — machinery less expensive than IPE but used for the same purposes.

Special Tooling. Jigs, dies, tools, taps, gauges, and other fixtures used for special fabrication are defined as special tooling. The key point here is that the use must be for specialty items. If the tooling can be used to build any common part, it is not special tooling.

Special Test Equipment (STE). STE consists of single or multipurpose test units designed to accomplish special testing. As was the case with special tooling, STE must not be usable for general purpose work. A common oscilloscope does not qualify as STE.

Government Furnished Material (GFM). GFM consists of anything that is incorporated into the end item, thereby losing its original identity.

Military Property. This category encompasses anything used to injure or threaten the enemy such as armored vehicles or guns.

Inventory Management

Does the company have an inventory management system for adequately controlling material, special tooling, special test equipment, plant equipment, real property, and military property? (See DAR APP B-101, 103, 201, 202, 300, 306, 400, 501, 502, DAR 7-104.24, 7-104.28, 7-203.21, and DAR Sup 3.) The company is required to establish and maintain a control system by type of property in its possession. The provisions of DAR require specific minimum requirements for information on government property to be contained on the records. The contractor is also required to control contractor-owned supplies during handling, storage, and shipment to protect the quality of products and prevent damage, loss, deterioration, degradation, or substitution of products. An effective inventory management system should address the following areas:

- All assets should be promptly and properly classified, identified, and labeled.
- Adequate inventory control records should be kept for each type of property.
- Adequate move order system should be in effect.
- Accurate locator records should be kept.
- Segregation of government-owned property versus contractor-owned property.
- Preservation and periodic inspection of property in storage for deterioration or critical environment control.
- Safeguarding property against theft.
- Control and accountability for returnable and reusable containers.
- Method used to ensure reasonable consumption of materials.
- System of first-in/first-out for materials subject to age deterioration or warranty expirations.
- Adequate control of assets transferred between programs or contracts.
- Physical inventories conducted according to contractual requirements or periodically, as specified.

Incident Reporting

Does the company provide for timely and accurate reporting of loss, damage, or destruction of government property and initiation of corrective action to prevent recurrence? (See DAR App B-101, 203, DAR 7-104.24, and 7-203.21.) The company is required to report all cases of loss, damage, or destruction of government property in its possession or control to the property administrator as soon as such facts become known or when requested by the property administrator. The contractor must take all reasonable steps to protect damaged government property from further loss or damage. Loss, damage, or destruction of government property caused by perils such as mysterious disappearance, employee negligence, or theft require corrective action by the company to prevent recurrence of such incidents.

Effective Maintenance

Does the company's system provide for an effective maintenance program for government property? (See DAR App B-602, DAR 7-104.28, 7-702.14, and AFSCR 78-5.) The company should have a preventive maintenance program for government property ensuring that required maintenance is performed regularly. The preventive maintenance program includes, but is not limited to, periodic inspection of all government property, protection by proper storage and preservation methods, and regularly scheduled lubrication. The company should have adequate records disclosing maintenance actions performed and deficiencies observed, and that provide for the following:

- Publishing a current normal maintenance plan.
- Maintenance records reflecting actions completed, including costs and description of work done.
- A maintenance plan requiring technical order compliance on government property.
- A maintenance plan requiring inspection by technically qualified personnel.
- A maintenance plan including provisions for highlighting high maintenance cost items for review and corrective action by management.
- A maintenance plan establishing acceptable minimum preventive maintenance standards that include specific intervals for all government property requiring maintenance.

Disposition

Does the company have a system for promptly identifying, reporting, and disposing of excess government property and identifying idle contractor-owned property? (See DAR App B-101, 106, 202, 303, DAR 7-104.24, 7-203.21, 24-201, 24-203, 24-203.6, 24-204, 24-205, 24-206, 24-302.2, 24-302.4, 24-302.5, 24-302.6, 24-302.8, 24-302.9, 24-210, and AFM 78-9.) The company should have provisions to identify and report *excess* government property. In addition, the company's system should provide for identifying and reporting *idle* contractor-owned property and appropriate treatment of associated costs. The company's documented system should provide for the following:

- A system for reviewing each type of asset in its possession to identify excess government-owned property and idle contractor-owned property.
- A system for diverting to other work or returning contractor-acquired property to suppliers for appropriate credit.
- A system for taking appropriate steps to report excess property.
- A system for appropriate disposition of excess and surplus property.
- A method to accomplish sales of surplus contractor inventory.
- Shipping instructions and contractual requirements pertaining to packaging, crating, handling, and transportation that will be properly implemented.
- A system to effectively manage accumulation and disposal of scrap.
- A method of controlling specialty metals (gold, silver, platinum) and high value items (items costing $1,000 or more).

References

1. Pascarella, Perry. "Management of Quality and the Quality of Management." *Industry Week,* 10 January 1983.
2. Senia, Al M. "Can Business Ethics Turn on U.S. Industry?" *Iron Age,* 10 November 1982.
3. Benner, Susan. "Peter's Principles: Secrets of Growth." *Inc.,* July 1983.
4. Livingston, W. C. "Status Report for White House Conference on Productivity." 6 June 1983.
5. Ouchi, William. *Theory Z.* Mass.: Addison-Wesley Publishing Co., 1981.
6. Acknowledgement is made to General Dynamics, Hewlett-Packard, and Texas Instruments for use of their Policy Statements.
7. Harrison, James C., Jr. "How to Stay on Top of the Job." *Harvard Business Review,* November-December 1961.
8. Thurauf, Robert J. *Management Auditing.* New York: AMACOM, 1980.
9. Wachmak, R. "Participative Audit — A New Management Tool." International Conference on Quality Control, Tokyo, 1978.
10. "AFCMD Regulation 178-1." Headquarters Air Force Contract Management Division, Kirtland Air Force Base, NM, 30 July 1981.
11. Talley, D. J. "General Dynamics QIP." Mission Assurance Conference, Los Angeles, Calif., 1983.
12. Odiarne, George S. "Three Keys to Professional Supervision." *Manage,* May 1983.
13. Coburn, Jim. "General Dynamics Quality Assurance Pathfinder Proposal." 6 May 1974.
14. *Government Contract Audits.* American Graduate University and Procurement Associations Inc., Course Outline Brochure, October 1983.
15. Hershman, Arlene and Henreiette Sender. "Cooking the Books." *Dun's Business Month,* January 1983.
16. Sirovy, Loel J. "The Organization." *Quality,* August 1980.
17. Brewer, C. S. and M. Howell. "Managing the Company Wide Quality Manual." *Quality,* June 1983.
18. White, Bruce. "Measuring the Status of Quality." *Quality,* August 1983.
19. "Quality Cost System Questionnaire." *Quality Progress,* April 1983.
20. Campanella, Jack and F. J. Conoran. "Principles of Quality Costs." *Quality Progress,* April 1983.
21. Talley, D. J. "Helping Suppliers Meet Your SPECs." *Contract Management,* November 1981.
22. Carpenter, C. L. Management Training Seminar, ASQC Section 1416, Euless, Texas, 15 February 1984.
23. Beck, A. C., Jr. and E. D. Hillmar. *A Practical Approach to Organizational Development Through MBO.* Mass.: Addison-Wesley Publishing Co. 1972.
24. Cathey, Paul. "Industry's Man in the Middle." *Iron Age,* 21 January 1983.
25. Berry, B. H. and B. H. Le Cerf. "Nisson's Track Plant: People and Pilots Under One Roof." *Iron Age,* 15 September 1982.

26. Garrett, I. E., Jr. "Chairman's Message." *Manage,* May 1983.
27. *Value Engineering.* Guidebook for Department of Defense Contractors, Defense Logistics Agency, August 1982.
28. *Cost Reduction Program.* General Dynamics Fort Worth Division, SP 2.20, December 1979.
29. "Transition of Weapons Systems from Development to Production." Report of Defense Science Board Office of Under Secretary of Defense Research and Engineering, Pentagon, Washington, DC, August 1983.
30. Irving, Robert R. "Quality In Design." *Iron Age,* 1 August 1983.
31. Bear, J. C. Engineering Quality Improvement Program Training at General Dynamics Pomona Division, Presentation at 4th International Conference on Reliability and Maintainability, 21-25 May 1984, Lannion, France.
32. Martin, Charles C. *Project Management: How to Make It Work.* New York, NY: AMACOM 1976.
33. "Transition from Development to Production." DOD Directive 4245.7, Deputy Chief of Naval Material (R,M&Q), Washington, DC.
34. Juran, J. M., Dr. Frank M. Gryna, Jr., and R. S., Binghan, Jr., *Quality Control Handbook.* New York, N. Y.,: McGraw-Hill Co., 1974.
35. Brusman, Calvin. "Subcontracting Made Easy." *Contract Management,* September 1983.
36. Pettit, R. E. "Vendor Evaluation Made Simple." *Quality Progress,* March 1984.
37. Talley, D. J. "Helping Suppliers Meet Your SPECs." *Contract Management,* November 1981.
38. *Manufacturing Management.* Handbook for Program Managers, DOD, Defense Systems Management College, Fort Belvoir, Va., January 1982.
39. *Manufacturing Management.* Handbook for Program Managers, DOD, Defense Systems Management College, Fort Belvoir, Va., January 1982.
40. Woo, Carolyn Y. and Arnold C. Cooper. "The Surprising Case for Low Market Share." *Harvard Business Review,* November-December 1982.
41. MacMillan, Ian C. "Preemptive Strategies." *Harvard Business Review,* 6: 1 (Spring 1984).
42. Rindner, Corey. "GFP From the PCO's Perspective." *Contract Management,* 25:10 (October 1985).

APPENDIX A QUALITY AWARENESS OPINION SURVEY

Quality Improvement Program — Employee Opinion Survey

First, thank you for volunteering to participate in this employee opinion survey. Your input, along with that from your fellow employees, will provide direction to the quality improvement target areas. You know the activities of your group and can point out the problem areas.

We need your help.

- Improving quality and productivity are *essential* company goals. They will have a large impact on company business and available jobs for you, the employees. We plan to implement a long-term, total systems approach.
- These improvements will require some changes in many portions of our work systems; changes in methods, materials, machines, management, etc.
- The success of the effort will depend on identifying areas where significant gains in quality and productivity can be made. Your input will be used to identify those areas.

Frankness is very important.

- Please answer the attached questionnaire carefully and honestly. Your anonymity will be fully protected. Only honest answers can provide a clear picture of where we are and what we need to do to improve.
- The responses we receive will be summarized to provide an indication of the key areas which need to be worked. Actions will be developed to remove the barriers to quality and productivity identified in this survey.
- Should you wish to add comments beyond the questions on any given page, please feel free to do so. A space is provided. If necessary, use the back of the page.

Survey Categories

- Policy
- Quality Practices
- Organizational Structure
- Work Assignments
- Resources
- Skills and Knowledge
- Work Groups and Departments
- Decision Making
- Feedback
- Job Satisfaction
- Human Resource
  Development
- Incentives and Recognition
- Quality Promotion
- Supervisor and Employee
  Relations
- Improvement Opportunities

Subject: *Quality Policy* — A company's reputation for quality products can be reached more easily if its management has clearly conveyed to all of the employees the overall quality policy and the standards or specifications applicable to the product manufactured or the services rendered.

Please answer the two questions below based on your experience.

Statement	Question 1					Question 2				
	How does each statement in the left-hand column apply to your personal experience?					How important do you think the subject of each statement is to your particular work situation?				
	Seldom		Sometimes		Usually	Not Very Important		Somewhat Important		Very Important
	1	2	3	4	5	1	2	3	4	5
1. There is available to me a clear statement of my company's policy in regard to the quality of our product.	1	2	3	4	5	1	2	3	4	5
2. I have written specifications and/or standards readily available to me that define what a quality product or a quality service is *for my particular job.*	1	2	3	4	5	1	2	3	4	5
3. My supervisor observes the company quality policy and adheres to the requirements of the work specifications and standards.	1	2	3	4	5	1	2	3	4	5
4. I feel comfortable with the quality of the products and/or services of my department.	1	2	3	4	5	1	2	3	4	5

Comments:

Subject: *Quality Practices* — If a quality policy is to be meaningful, it is important that the actual practices are consistent with the policy statements.

Please answer the two questions below based on your experience.

Factors	Question 1 What type of performance or day-to-day practice seems most important to your supervisor: i.e., if you were to be complimented on your work, which factor in the left-hand column usually carries the most weight? (circle one answer)	Question 2 If you could choose only one (1) of the five (5) factors in the left hand column, which one would you personally consider most important? (circle one answer)
1. Quality of the work.	1	1
2. Making the work schedule.	2	2
3. Cutting costs.	3	3
4. All equally important.	4	4
5. I am not sure which one is considered most important.	5	5

Comments:

Subject: *Organizational Structure* — Organizational structures are designed to provide for smooth allocation and flow of resources (e.g., authority, decisions, information, personnel, materials, etc.) to facilitate productivity.

Please answer the two questions below based on your experience.

Elements	Question 1 Over the course of the past year how has each element in the left-hand column applied to your personal situation?					Question 2 How important is it that each of the elements be met, most of the time?				
	Seldom		Sometimes		Usually	Not Very Important		Somewhat Important		Very Important
1. I understand my authority within my organization.	1	2	3	4	5	1	2	3	4	5
2. I understand what results I am accountable for on an assignment.	1	2	3	4	5	1	2	3	4	5
3. I know exactly to whom I report for assignments.	1	2	3	4	5	1	2	3	4	5
4. I know who appraises my performance on assignments.	1	2	3	4	5	1	2	3	4	5
5. I have sufficient authority to perform my assignments.	1	2	3	4	5	1	2	3	4	5
6. Problems are tackled when they arise as opposed to being pushed aside or re-directed to a higher level.	1	2	3	4	5	1	2	3	4	5
7. The general feeling among the people in my organization generally reflects pride in the organization and respect for the management.	1	2	3	4	5	1	2	3	4	5

Comments:

Subject: *Work Assignments* — The products or services you provide and the manner in which you are directed to carry out the tasks involved.

Please answer the two questions below based on your experience.

Factors	Question 1 — What has been your experience in regard to work assignments you are given by your supervisor?					Question 2 — How would you personally rate the importance of each of the factors as they apply to the work assignments you are given?				
	Seldom		Sometimes		Usually	Not Very Important		Somewhat Important		Very Important
1. I understand what I am to accomplish.	1	2	3	4	5	1	2	3	4	5
2. Written instructions regarding what is expected are provided.	1	2	3	4	5	1	2	3	4	5
3. I am given assignments appropriate to my level of ability and experience.	1	2	3	4	5	1	2	3	4	5
4. I understand how the quality of my work will be judged.	1	2	3	4	5	1	2	3	4	5
5. I understand how my work will be judged in terms of meeting schedule.	1	2	3	4	5	1	2	3	4	5
6. Assignments are well planned — I am not continually pulled off one assignment to work another.	1	2	3	4	5	1	2	3	4	5
7. My assignments are interesting and challenge my ability.	1	2	3	4	5	1	2	3	4	5

Comments:

Appendix A

Subject: *Resources* — The things needed to help you complete work assignments. They include supplies, tools, information, help from other people, access to decision makers, authority, etc.

Please answer the two questions below based on your experience.

Factors	Question 1 — What has been your experience in regard to each of the factors in the left-hand column in regard to completing your work assignments in a *quality* fashion, in the time prescribed?					Question 2 — How important do you think each of the factors is in your particular case?				
	Seldom		Sometimes		Usually	Not Very Important		Somewhat Important		Very Important
1. The facilities and equipment available to me are adequate.	1	2	3	4	5	1	2	3	4	5
2. Sufficient supplies are readily available to me.	1	2	3	4	5	1	2	3	4	5
3. I am given adequate time to complete the majority of assignments.	1	2	3	4	5	1	2	3	4	5
4. The personnel I am assigned or work with are competent to help complete the assignment.	1	2	3	4	5	1	2	3	4	5
5. Available information and/or data is provided in time to help complete the majority of assignments.	1	2	3	4	5	1	2	3	4	5
6. I have ready access to key decision makers for timely, higher level decisions, when required.	1	2	3	4	5	1	2	3	4	5
For supervisors and managers only:										
7. I am provided with adequate budget or manpower to complete the majority of tasks.	1	2	3	4	5	1	2	3	4	5

Comments:

Subject: *Skills and Knowledge* — Provisions that are made for employees to learn or upgrade the things they need to know in order to perform effectively.

Please answer the two questions below based on your experience.

Factors	Question 1 — What has been your experience in regard to each of the skills and knowledge factors in the left-hand column?					Question 2 — How important do you think each factor is to the quality of the work output of any department or section?				
	Seldom		Sometimes		Usually	Not Very Important		Somewhat Important		Very Important
	1	2	3	4	5	1	2	3	4	5
1. I have the technical skills and knowledge to do a quality job in my assignments.	1	2	3	4	5	1	2	3	4	5
2. When I need additional training in skills/knowledge, I can get it.	1	2	3	4	5	1	2	3	4	5
3. When a quality problem arises, I have the general ability to *recognize* it.	1	2	3	4	5	1	2	3	4	5
4. Likewise, I have the general ability to *analyze* it.	1	2	3	4	5	1	2	3	4	5
5. Next, I have the general ability to *develop* a *solution* to the problem.	1	2	3	4	5	1	2	3	4	5
6. In working out the solution, I have the ability to express my viewpoint(s) clearly.	1	2	3	4	5	1	2	3	4	5
7. Skill training is an important issue in my department/section.	1	2	3	4	5	1	2	3	4	5
8. I have respect for the instructors assigned to training functions I have attended.	1	2	3	4	5	1	2	3	4	5

Comments:

Appendix A

Subject: *Work Groups/Departments* — To achieve a reputation for high quality work output at the section or department level, there has to be a reasonably clear definition of the mission, the role of the individual and the amount of training available.

Please answer the two questions below based on your experience.

Dept. No. _____

Factors	Question 1					Question 2				
	What has been your experience with regard to each of the factors listed in the left-hand column?					How important do you think each factor is in terms of contributing to the "quality of work" reputation of the department?				
	Seldom		Sometimes		Usually	Not Very Important		Somewhat Important		Very Important
1. The goal/mission of the department and section is clear to the majority of people in the department.	1	2	3	4	5	1	2	3	4	5
2. My individual role is clear to me.	1	2	3	4	5	1	2	3	4	5
3. Training is an important issue in the department/section and is available to those who need it.	1	2	3	4	5	1	2	3	4	5
4. The department/section gets recognition for its efforts.	1	2	3	4	5	1	2	3	4	5
5. Quality of output is stressed from the top level of management to first line supervision.	1	2	3	4	5	1	2	3	4	5
6. Individuals who do well get ready recognition.	1	2	3	4	5	1	2	3	4	5
7. Individuals who do little or no productive work get reprimanded.	1	2	3	4	5	1	2	3	4	5
8. The department/section responds well when a crisis situation arises.	1	2	3	4	5	1	2	3	4	5
9. I feel that I make an important contribution to my department's mission.	1	2	3	4	5	1	2	3	4	5

Comments:

Subject: *Decision Making* — The extent to which you are involved in decisions that affect your work assignments or the use of resources.

Please answer the two questions below based on your experience.

Statements	Question 1 How many times last year was each statement in the left-hand column applicable to your work situation?					Question 2 How important do you think each statement is to maintaining a good work attitude?				
	Seldom	Sometimes			Usually	Not Very Important		Somewhat Important		Very Important
1. My input is requested in the decisions affecting my job.	1	2	3	4	5	1	2	3	4	5
2. This input is requested *before* the decision is made and not *after*.	1	2	3	4	5	1	2	3	4	5
3. I am told why a decision was made the way it was.	1	2	3	4	5	1	2	3	4	5
4. I am free to use my own judgment about the way I apply resources, supplies, or equipment.	1	2	3	4	5	1	2	3	4	5
5. I am permitted to make appropriate decisions on my own initiative.	1	2	3	4	5	1	2	3	4	5

Comments:

Subject: *Feedback* — (Complaints or compliments) from your supervisor, or from people you work with closely, that gives you some idea of what others think of the quality of your work.

Please answer the two questions below based on your experience.

Statements	Question 1: Over the course of the past year, how has each of the statements in the left-hand column applied to your work situation?					Question 2: How important do you think it is that you receive feedback as it is described in the left-hand column?				
	Seldom		Sometimes		Usually	Not Very Important		Somewhat Important		Very Important
From my supervisor:										
1. I get verbal or written feedback on each completed assignment.	1	2	3	4	5	1	2	3	4	5
2. The feedback is timely enough to allow me the opportunity to improve the quality of the work.	1	2	3	4	5	1	2	3	4	5
3. Someone else checks the quality of my work before it leaves the area.	1	2	3	4	5	1	2	3	4	5
4. The feedback I get is specific and helps me know what was right or wrong and why.	1	2	3	4	5	1	2	3	4	5
5. I consider the feedback useful in understanding how to improve my performance.	1	2	3	4	5	1	2	3	4	5
6. The manner in which the feedback is given is courteous and not aggravating.	1	2	3	4	5	1	2	3	4	5
From other people:										
7. When I work with others, I get complaints or compliments on the quality of my work.	1	2	3	4	5	1	2	3	4	5

Comments:

Subject: *Job Satisfaction* — Generally reflected by the enthusiasm with which a person approaches his or her work and the general satisfaction with quality of assignments completed.

Please answer the two questions below based on your experience.

Factors	Question 1 — What has been your experience with regard to each of the factors in the left-hand column over a typical year's period?					Question 2 — How important do you think each factor is in terms of influencing the quality of the work output?				
	Seldom		Sometimes		Usually	Not Very Important		Somewhat Important		Very Important
1. My day-to-day assignments provide job satisfaction.	1	2	3	4	5	1	2	3	4	5
2. My assignments meet my needs for personal development.	1	2	3	4	5	1	2	3	4	5
3. My supervisor is a positive influence on my general attitude.	1	2	3	4	5	1	2	3	4	5
4. I have respect for the people I work with.	1	2	3	4	5	1	2	3	4	5
5. The people I work with share ideas to improve the quality of the department or group output.	1	2	3	4	5	1	2	3	4	5
6. Back and forth communication with my supervisor is easy and comfortable.	1	2	3	4	5	1	2	3	4	5
7. I approach my work with a high degree of enthusiasm.	1	2	3	4	5	1	2	3	4	5
8. The people around me have respect for their supervision.	1	2	3	4	5	1	2	3	4	5

Comments:

Appendix A

Subject: *Human Resource Development* — A company's success depends largely on how well it selects and develops its people.

Based on your experience, please indicate your opinion in regard to the following statements:

Statements	No Opinion	Strongly Disagree	Disagree	Agree	Strongly Agree
1. Selection criteria for employment are adequate to assure acquisition of new employees who are generally well qualified and willing to provide quality products or services.	1	2	3	4	5
2. Selection criteria for promotions or merit increases are based on an individual's actual performance rather than subjective criteria, such as personal likes or dislikes, or years of service.	1	2	3	4	5
3. Before being placed on a new job, a person receives enough training to ensure that he or she will be successful in regard to meeting the quality requirements of the new job.	1	2	3	4	5
4. There is an effective development program in place that helps people upgrade their skills and technical knowledge so they may compete for positions they would like to have.	1	2	3	4	5
5. Company policy encourages an individual to undertake personal improvement through participation in either company-sponsored classes or those elected by the individual on his or her own initiative.	1	2	3	4	5

Comments:

151

Subject: *Incentives/Recognition* — Excluding salary consideration, indications that the quality of your work is appreciated and/or that your contribution is of value to the overall organization.

Please answer the two questions below based on your experience.

Factors	Question 1					Question 2
	Please indicate *your actual* experience with regard to the frequency of occurrence for each factor in the left-hand column.					How would you *rank* the factors in terms of importance to you personally? (Rank the factors 1 thru 6, no. 1 being the most important.)
	Never	Very Rare	Some-times	Frequent	Always	
1. Direct verbal or written complaints from my immediate supervisor.	1	2	3	4	5	◯
2. Certificates of appreciation from the general manager.	1	2	3	4	5	◯
3. Direct verbal or written compliments from the department head.	1	2	3	4	5	◯
4. Merchandise awards.	1	2	3	4	5	◯
5. Expressions of respect from associate workers on my level.	1	2	3	4	5	◯
6. Citations (with name) in the company paper.	1	2	3	4	5	◯

Comments:

Subject: *Quality Promotion* — Actions taken generally at the management or supervisory level to keep the entire work force aware of what the customer (or user) thinks of the quality level of products or services.

Please answer the two questions below based on your experience.

Question 1	Question 2
What real interest do you take in each of the items in the left-hand column as a means of keeping you aware of our customer's opinion of our quality levels?	Would you please use the space below to give brief opinion(s) on how we could improve "top down" communications to the work force and thereby upgrade quality awareness?

Items	Seldom Interested		Somewhat Interested		Very Interested	Your Ideas
1. Articles in company papers, periodicals, or other publications about quality.	1	2	3	4	5	
2. Posters displayed in various areas of the plant on the subject of quality.	1	2	3	4	5	
3. Monthly award ceremonies recognizing the quality winner of the month.	1	2	3	4	5	
4. Scrap and rework cost charts posted in various departments.	1	2	3	4	5	
5. Letters of commendation from Air Force officials on product quality performance.	1	2	3	4	5	

Comments:

Subject: *Supervisor/Employee Relations* — The compatibility factor and/or the relationship between the employee and his or her supervisor has a significant influence on the quality level of the output of a department or work group.

Based on your experience, please indicate your opinion in regard to the following statements.

Statements	Poor	Below Average	Average	Above Average	Exceptional
1. In my opinion, my immediate supervisor would rate *my* quality performance as:	1	2	3	4	5
2. In terms of the following characteristics, I would rate my immediate supervisor as follows:					
A. Technical Knowledge	1	2	3	4	5
B. Administrative Skill	1	2	3	4	5
C. Ability to Communicate	1	2	3	4	5
D. Enthusiasm	1	2	3	4	5
E. Availability	1	2	3	4	5
F. Quality Consciousness	1	2	3	4	5
G. Decision-Making Ability	1	2	3	4	5
H. Problem-Solving Ability	1	2	3	4	5
3. In my opinion, the group I work with would give the supervisor an overall rating of:	1	2	3	4	5

Comments:

APPENDIX B
MANAGEMENT
ASSESSMENT
PROGRAM

Subject: *Improvement Opportunities* — Quality and productivity can always be improved with everyone working toward common goals. Instead of management telling you what *we* think needs improvement, we want *you* to tell *us*. The space below is for that purpose. Please use it.

Department _____ This is your opportunity to identify departmental practices, systems, or procedures where significant improvements need to be made to upgrade the quality of the product or associated services.

Note: If additional space is required, please use the back of this page.

Area / Functional Area Question	Organization						Supervisor	Dates (Now / Next Audit)		Closed
	Existence		Adequate		Compliance		By	Correction Required		
								Task Team Required	Response Due Date	Sat. Date
	Y	N	Y	N	Y	N				
GM-1										
a. Does the organization have a strategic plan that looks 5-20 years into the future?										
b. Does the organization have an adequate yearly operating plan with quarterly objectives?										
c. Does the organization have a management-by-objectives program?										
d. Does the organization have a variable, in-depth, documented MIS system that is both upward and downward looking?										
e. Does the organization have a formal QIP that addresses the major product quality and cost areas?										
f. Does the organization have formal supervisory selection systems that have a basis of technical, administrative, and interpersonal skills?										

Area	Organization						Supervisor	Dates			
		Existence		Adequate		Compliance		Correction Required		Now	Closed
										Next Audit	
Functional Area Question		Y	N	Y	N	Y	N	By	Task Team Required	Response Due Date	Sat. Date
GM-2											
a. Does the organization have a system for analyzing contracts and sales orders and assigning responsibility for fulfilling these requirements?											
b. Does the organization have an internal audit system to ensure that financial authorities are exercised within prescribed limitations and good business practices?											
c. Does the organization have a system for reporting to executive levels all significant financial management commitments and decisions?											
d. Does the organization have a system which identifies how the company/department determines and implements manpower requirements and uses the manpower to satisfy present or projected business (contractual) commitments?											

Page _____ of _____ Pages

Area	Organization						Supervisor	Dates		
		Existence		Adequate		Compliance	By		Now	
									Next Audit	
Functional Area Question		Y	N	Y	N	Y	N		Correction Required	Closed
									Task Team Required	Response Due Date	Sat. Date

GM-3

a. Does the organization have a product assurance department that will act for the general manager and implement a total quality program?

b. Does the organization identify all quality program contractual requirements and assign authority and responsibility for their accomplishment?

c. Does the organization provide that some management organization continually review the status and adequacy of the quality program and track the required corrective action?

Area: Organization   Supervisor   Dates

Page ___ of ___ Pages

Functional Area Question	Existence		Adequate		Compliance		By	Correction Required		Closed
	Y	N	Y	N	Y	N		Task Team Required	Response Due Date (Now / Next Audit)	Sat. Date
QA-1										
a. Does the quality assurance manager have the authority and organizational freedom (report to general manager) to exercise top management's dictates?										
b. Does the quality organization have a good policy/procedure system IAW MIL-Q-9858A and other customer requirements?										
c. Do the quality assurance documented procedures define the methods of feedback to other departments?										
d. Does the organization have a total quality cost collection system that is used by top management?										
e. Does the organization's quality system provide for a closed-loop, corrective action feedback to other departments and management?										
f. Does the organization have an effective metrology and calibration system IAW MIL-STD-45662?										

Appendix B

Area	Organization						Supervisor	Dates		
								Now		
								Next Audit		
Functional Area Question	Existence		Adequate		Compliance		By	Correction Required		Closed
	Y	N	Y	N	Y	N		Task Team Required	Response Due Date	Sat. Date
QA-1 (cont'd) g. Does the organization have adequate control of the quality of purchased materials/products? h. Does the organization have an organized, disciplined approach to acquisition, development, and maintenance of software (MIL-STD-52779A)?										

Functional Area Question	Organization						Supervisor	Correction Required		
Area	Existence		Adequate		Compliance		By	Task Team Required	Response Due Date	Closed Sat. Date
	Y	N	Y	N	Y	N				Dates: Now / Next Audit
IR-1										
a. Do you review your human resources in total system terms?										
b. Does the company have an MBO appraisal system and does the industrial relations department flow these out to the departments for the yearly planning?										
c. Does the company/division have an effective training program?										
d. Does the company have an effective hiring program?										
e. Does management have a program to communicate to the people their benefits and their relationship to the company's health?										
f. Does the company have a documented safety program to prevent mishaps that result in an increase in cost, program/project impact, or loss or damage to human life?										

Page   of   Pages

Page ___ of ___ Pages

Area	Organization						Supervisor	Dates	Correction Required			
	Existence		Adequate		Compliance						Now	Next Audit
Functional Area Question							By		Task Team Required	Response Due Date	Closed Sat. Date
	Y	N	Y	N	Y	N					
FIN-1											
a. Does the company have documented procedures for identifying and describing responsibilities and authorities to be assigned to each functional area?											
b. Does the company have an adequate system for managing and controlling indirect costs?											
c. Does the company have adequate controls to optimize cash flow, both paying and collecting?											
d. Does the company have an adequate system for tracking direct budgeted costs and schedule versus actual performance?											
e. Does the company have an effective cost reduction and value control program?											

Page ___ of ___ Pages

Area	Organization			Supervisor	Dates		
						Now	
						Next Audit	

Functional Area Question	Existence		Adequate		Compliance		By	Correction Required		Response Due Date	Closed Sat. Date
	Y	N	Y	N	Y	N		Task Team Required			
ENGR-1											
a. Does the company have documented engineering objectives and policies which clearly define the engineering management system, and are they approved by the chief operating official?											
b. Does the company have an adequate design management system?											
c. Does the company have an adequate reliability management system?											
d. Does the contractor have an adequate maintainability management system?											
e. Does the company have an active, traceable value engineering (VE) management system?											
f. Does the contractor have an adequate test management system?											

Area											
	Organization						Supervisor		Dates Now		
									Next Audit		
		Existence		Adequate		Compliance		Correction Required			Closed
Functional Area Question											Sat. Date
		Y	N	Y	N	Y	N	By	Task Team Required	Response Due Date	
ENGR-1 (cont'd)											
g. Does the contractor have an adequate system safety engineering management system?											
h. Does the contractor have an adequate configuration management system?											
i. Does the company have an engineering quality improvement training program?											

Area	Organization						Supervisor	Dates		
									Now	
									Next Audit	
Functional Area Question	Existence		Adequate		Compliance		By	Correction Required		Closed Sat. Date
								Task Team Required	Response Due Date	
	Y	N	Y	N	Y	N				
PM-1										
a. Does the contractor have a documented program management system?										
b. Does the company have a development training program for program manager?										
c. Does the program manager know, have a listing of, and visit schedule for the customer?										
d. Does the program manager have a MIS to report significant problems, cost, schedule, quality, or technical status to appropriate management levels?										
e. Is the program manager really using innovative methods?										

Appendix B

Area	Organization						Supervisor		Dates		Page ___ of ___ Pages
	Functional Area Question	Existence	Adequate	Compliance			Correction Required			Now	Closed
		Y	N	Y	N	Y	N	By	Task Team Required	Response Due Date	Next Audit	Sat. Date

PROC/SUB-1

a. Does the company have current procurement policies, written and covering all functions participating in acquisition management?

b. Does the company have an effective, formal, and documented system for determining and controlling precontractual actions?

c. Does the contractor have an adequate system for developing purchase requirements and source selection?

d. Does the company have an adequate system for cost and price analysis that meets the criteria of Armed Services Pricing Manual #1 (ASPM-1)?

e. Does the company have an adequate documented system for management of subcontractors that provides visibility of cost, schedule, performance, and a means to validate subcontract status?

167

Page   of   Pages

Area	Organization						Supervisor	Dates		
									Now	
									Next Audit	
Functional Area Question	Existence		Adequate		Compliance		By	Correction Required		Closed
								Task Team Required	Response Due Date	Sat. Date
	Y	N	Y	N	Y	N				
PD-1										
a. Are the authorities and responsibilities in the company's documented system for managing manufacturing operations complete, properly identified, assigned, and implemented?										
b. Does the company have an adequate manufacturing planning system?										
c. Does manufacturing adequately use an integrated work measurement/methods improvement system to control production costs and productivity?										
d. Does the company have an adequate system for forecasting, scheduling, and controlling workloads?										
e. Does the company have an adequate packaging, handling, and transportability system?										

Appendix B

Area	Organization						Supervisor		Dates		Page of Pages	

Now / Next Audit

Functional Area Question	Existence		Adequate		Compliance		By	Correction Required Task Team Required	Response Due Date	Closed Sat. Date
	Y	N	Y	N	Y	N				
LOG/CS-1										
a. Does the company have an adequate integrated logistics support management system?										
b. Does the company have a logistics plan to meet the needs of the product program?										
c. Does the company have an adequate organization and staff to accomplish the logistics and customer support service?										
d. Has the company adequately assessed the vendor's role in the logistics lifeline?										

Area	Organization						Supervisor	Dates	Page of Pages
		Existence	Adequate	Compliance					Now / Next Audit
Functional Area Question		Y / N	Y / N	Y / N	By	Correction Required: Task Team Required	Response Due Date		Closed Sat. Date

MKT/PLNG-1

a. Are marketing management efforts directed to accomplishing the strategic and operating plans?

b. Is market research management capable of dynamic tactics during the product(s) life cycle?

c. Are long-range sales quotas established for (1) products or product lines, (2) sales or geographic areas, and (3) salespersons?

d. Is advertising management capable of developing a well-thought-out and well-integrated advertising program?

e. Is the physical distribution an integral part of long-range marketing plans?

Appendix B

Page ___ of ___ Pages

Area	Organization						Supervisor	Dates		
								Now		
								Next Audit		

Functional Area Question	Existence		Adequate		Compliance		By	Correction Required		Closed Sat. Date
	Y	N	Y	N	Y	N		Task Team Required	Response Due Date	
CON/EST-1										
a. Are the authorities and responsibilities in the contractor's documented contract administration system complete, properly identified, assigned, and implemented?										
b. Does the company have an estimating system which provides accurate, complete, and timely price proposals?										
c. Does the company have an adequate system for ensuring that overhead FPRA proposals and final overhead claims are timely and responsive?										
d. Does the company have a system for managing the various administrative requirements imposed by the recurring requirements of government contracts?										
e. Does the company have an adequate system for settlement of terminated contracts and subcontracts?										

171

Management Audits for Excellence

Area	Organization							Supervisor		Dates	Now		
		Existence		Adequate		Compliance					Next Audit		
Functional Area Question		Y	N	Y	N	Y	N	By	Correction Required	Task Team Required	Response Due Date	Closed Sat. Date

IPM-1

a. Are the authorities and responsibilities in the company's documented system for managing property complete, properly identified, assigned, and implemented?

b. Does the company have an inventory management system for adequately controlling material, special tooling, special test equipment, plant equipment, real property, and military property?

c. Does the company's system provide for timely and accurate reporting of incidents of loss, damage, or destruction of government property and initiation of corrective action to preclude recurrence?

d. Does the company's system provide for an effective maintenance program for government property?

172

Area	Organization						Supervisor	Dates	Page of Pages
		Existence		Adequate		Compliance			Now
									Next Audit
Functional Area Question		Y	N	Y	N	Y	N	By	Correction Required	
									Task Team Required	Response Due Date	Closed Sat. Date
IPM-1 (cont'd) e. Does the company have a system for promptly identifying, reporting, and disposing of excess government property and identifying idle contractor-owned property?											

Index